Leonardo's Kitchen Note Books

LEONARDO'S
KITCHEN
NOTE BOOKS

Leonardo da Vinci's
notes on cookery and
table etiquette

newly rendered into English
and edited by
SHELAGH and JONATHAN ROUTH

COLLINS
8 Grafton Street, London W1
1987

William Collins Sons and Co Ltd
London Glasgow Sydney Auckland
Toronto Johannesburg

BRITISH LIBRARY CATALOGUING IN PUBLICATION DATA

Leonardo, *da Vinci*
Leonardo's kitchen note books: Leonardo da Vinci's notes
on cookery and table etiquette.
1. Cookery, Italian
1. Title. 2. Routh, Shelagh. 3. Routh, Jonathan.
641.5945   TX723

ISBN 0-00-217165-1

Typeset by Ace Filmsetting Ltd, Frome Somerset
Made and printed in Great Britain by
William Collins Sons and Co Ltd, Glasgow

Designed by Marian Morris

CONTENTS

✦❀❀✦❀❀✦

The Codex Romanoff of Leonardo da Vinci

Cod. Atl. *in the text captions refers to the Codex Atlanticus in the Biblioteca Ambrosiana, Milan;* Ms.B *refers to the Mss. held in the Bibliotheque Nationale in Paris.*

ACKNOWLEDGMENTS

The Editors would like to express their thanks for the help given to them at various times by :

Professore Carlo Pietrangeli,
Direttore dei Musei Vaticani

Monsignor Russchoert,
Vice Prefetto di Biblioteca Apostolica

Monsignor Galbiati,
Direttore di Biblioteca Ambrosiana, Milano

Count Tino Vitteti
Count Pier-Francesco Calvi di Bergolo
Giovanella della Chiesa
Marchese Giovangeorgio Afan de Rivera
Carlo Alberto Lequio
Prince Nicolo Boncompagni-Ludovisi
Dado Torrigiani
Maureen Bonini
Marie-Louise Scio
Baranessa Magda Konopka
Antoinette Parks
William Thomson

and most especially they would like to thank Sra Scilla Marvino for her patient work of translation, not just from Italian to English, but also from the Latin to the Italian.

🎇 FOREWORD 🎇

by Dottore Marino Albinesi, Director of Public Prosecutions, Rome; President of the Circolo Enogastronomico d'Italia

It had always seemed odd that someone who was so curious about everything – as Leonardo da Vinci was – should have left so little record of any interest in food and cooking. This, the man whose greatest and best-known painting, that sparse culinary depiction called 'The Last Supper', and on which he spent three years of his life, was as much to do with food as with spiritual values. This, the man who, in his will, left a considerable portion of his estate to – of all persons – his *cook*, Battista de Villanis. This, the man who, throughout his life, was as heavily involved in food and cooking as he was in planning paintings and fortifications and investigating the countless other subjects which aroused his curiosity. In fact he was more *actively* involved in cooking than in any other subject. He had to be – not just as little more than a boy when, taking time off from his duties in Verrochio's studio, he worked for pocket money in the kitchens of a Florentine tavern; not just when, with Sandro Botticelli, he tried to run his own tavern; but most especially in his capacity as Master of the Revels and Feasting to the Sforza Court – a position, remember, that he filled for over thirteen years, and which would have had to involve him in a very considerable and first-hand knowledge of foodstuffs. And yet the amount of references to food and drink in the Note Books of Leonardo that we know to-day are minimal – a few generalizations, a few aphorisms, not a single mention or recipe from all his time with the Sforzas.

And now, in an attempt to fill this gap, we are presented with what an increasing number of people, and its present editors, refer to as the 'Codex Romanoff'. But even my old friend Shelagh Marvin Routh who with her husband Jonathan, has spent so many years in pursuit of this culinary indication of Leonardo, admit that there is absolutely no way whereby a copy manuscript typed in Italian, dealing almost exclusively with food, and which has apparently appeared out of nowhere* can be authenticated as a true copy of the original work of Leonardo da Vinci. What, even, are we meant to make of the brief note at its head: 'This is work which I, Pasquale Pisapia, have copied in longhand from the manuscript of Leonardo da Vinci now held at the Hermitage [Museum] in Leningrad' – ? Who was, or is, Pasquale Pisapia? How does it come about that he is, or was, the only person to know of the manuscript? And with officials at the Hermitage denying that any such work by Leonardo exists in their Museum it is a totally hapless task to seek out the manuscript's authenticity, let alone existence. (Though I readily admit the Russians have made other 'denials' in our time.) But let me also admit to why I believe the likelihood of there having been such a manuscript written by Leonardo is very real indeed.

    1. The very circumstances of Leonardo's life – his work in kitchens as a youth, his position of Master of the Revels and Feasting under the Sforzas, would have made it absolutely possible for him to have written these contents with authority.

    2. We must remember that of everything Leonardo wrote and drew probably little more than one third has survived to this day, the rest (like his known treatises on Horses and Architecture) has been lost, destroyed by fire or war, or simply disappeared (like the folios referred to as Codex

*I speak metaphorically, but until such time as the allegedly publicity-shy noble family of Piedmont, in whose possession the typescript is said to have been held since the last war, will come forward to give us some satisfactory explanation, 'nowhere' is the term I prefer to use.

Madrid which reappeared in the 1950s in the Biblioteca Nacional of Madrid having been mis-catalogued there for nearly 300 years).

3. We must remember, too, that the most part of what Leonardo wrote was of a fragmentary nature. On the same page of one of his Note Books might be four totally unrelated and unfinished thoughts, some written years after the others just because Leonardo may have found blank spaces on the page, some even written the reverse way up to the other entries. Leonardo's pupil Francesco Melzi, to whom he left all the Note Books (unless indeed King Francis I of France got away with any) went at them hard with scissors and paste to try and put them in some sort of order, as did Pompeio Leoni the sculptor and art dealer after him. (How much of the Folios might have remained on the cutting room floors during these processes one dreads to think.)

But the real point I am making here is that, given all these vicissitudes that the contents of the Note Books went through after Leonardo's death, there would have been plenty of scope for whole sections to have been stored in attics and forgotten about (there was a very thorough indifference to his writings to begin with), to have been appropriated, to have been misappropriated, later to have changed hands for money (remember King Charles of England's admonition to Lord Arundel to 'get me at any cost some of Leonard Vincent's writings,') remember the shady Count Guglielmo Libri who in 1868 'borrowed' a number of folios from the Bibliothèque Nationale in Paris, sold them to a Count Manzoni, whose heirs in 1892 sold them to – and here we get the start of the Russian connection – a Russian called Sabachnikoff (who subsequently returned only *some* of them to the Royal Library in Turin).

The matter was discussed at some length during the Biennale Enogastronomica Toscana held in Florence in 1982 shortly after the Codex Romanoff was first heard of. Most of my colleagues were agreed that the work *could* have been by

Leonardo. And the theory I really preferred – I believe it was il Conte de Rham's – was that the Codex went to Russia at the same time as one of the two Leonardo paintings now in the Hermitage Museum (and which the Russians do not deny they own). The slightly dubious Madonna Litta had been acquired from the great Visconti family of Milan by Czar Alexander II in 1865 and placed there. The more believable Madonna del Fiore was placed there by Czar Nicholas II in 1914. He had acquired it from the Benois family who had bought it from Prince Kurakin – a known friend of Sabachnikoff.

And if there was this demand for Leonardo's paintings from the Romanoffs why shouldn't they also have been interested in his writings? Sabachnikoff had some. And without any doubt some had passed through the hands of the Viscontis.

Alas that we have to speculate and cannot know the truth. But of this I am convinced, the writings here show the hand of Leonardo, I repeat he would have had the knowledge and the opportunities to compose them, and just because we cannot see the originals of them should not stop us taking them as genuine – if we want to. After all, it was so with the Englishman Shakespeare.

LEONARDO IN THE KITCHEN

An Outline of his 'Gastronomic' Life

The most important clue to Leonardo's lifelong interest in food must lie in the circumstances of his very early years. He is born on April 15th, 1452, in Vinci near Florence, the love-child of Ser Piero da Vinci, a Florentine notary, and Caterina, a lady of Vinci. Some few months after the event his father marries a sixteen-year-old Florentine lady, and his mother weds an out-of-work pastrycook from Vinci, Accatabriga di Piero del Vacca. Leonardo grows up in both households, but it is from the 'gross, untidy and gluttonous' Accatabriga (Ser Piero's description), who showers him with sweetmeats, who inculcates in him the subtleties of the cooking hearth, who lets him model in marzipans which can be left to harden in the Tuscan sun, that Leonardo acquires the sweet tooth and besottedness with food that stays with him all his life and threatens the success of so many of his other activities. After the age of ten Leonardo sees little of his stepfather as his real father causes him to stay in Florence to grow up alongside his half-brothers, and with them receive the rudiments of a formal education (which does not, how-ever, extend to learning Latin; all his life Leonardo wrote and spoke 'working-class' Florentine). Then in 1469 Ser Piero apprentices his now vastly fat first son to Verrochio the sculptor-painter-engineer-goldsmith-mathematician   at whose studio in Florence Botticelli is also an apprentice.

Within the year Leonardo is in trouble. While diligently digesting – though also querying – everything that Ver-rochio teaches, he also spends his time stuffing himself with the sweetmeats his stepfather sends him. Verrochio decides to punish him for *crapulando* – guzzling. And the punishment is that Leonardo has to paint an angel in the left hand panel of the Baptism of Christ Verrochio is engaged in for the Church of San Salvi (and which now hangs in the Uffizi in Florence, completely dominated by Leonardo's angel). But from that time on Leonardo ceases to be the 'fat boy' mocked by his fellow apprentices.

After three years of this apprenticeship Leonardo has to stand on his own feet – although is still able to work out of Verrochio's studio. It is to eke out the little income he receives from the few commissions that Verrochio now allows him that he goes to work in the evenings serving food at the famous Tavern of the Three Snails by the Ponte Vecchio bridge in Florence.

Then, in the spring of 1473, following the mysterious death by poisoning of all cooks at the Three Snails, Leonardo is put in charge of the tavern's kitchens. Verrochio, who has just asked his pupil to collaborate with him on a Baptism of Christ painting, is not a little put out by this abrupt departure. But Leonardo is too excited by this new challenge in the Snails' kitchens to stay. For many months now he has been looking with distress and distaste at the *polenta* – or porridge – which, together with chunks of unrecognizable meats, is the staple fare of the place; and has already come to the conclusion that anything so dull-looking and tasteless cannot be considered one of the Great Dishes of the Renaissance which he knows is going on around him. As head cook he sets to work to 'civilize' the fare served at the Three Snails.

RIGHT: Leonardo's plan for assembling the 200-foot long replica of the Sforza Castello he constructed in the Castello court-yard of pre-cast cake – mostly blocks of porridge reinforced with nuts and raisins covered in multi-coloured marzipans – to celebrate Ludovico Sforza's marriage to Beatrice D'Este.
Cod. Atl. fol. 49v–b.

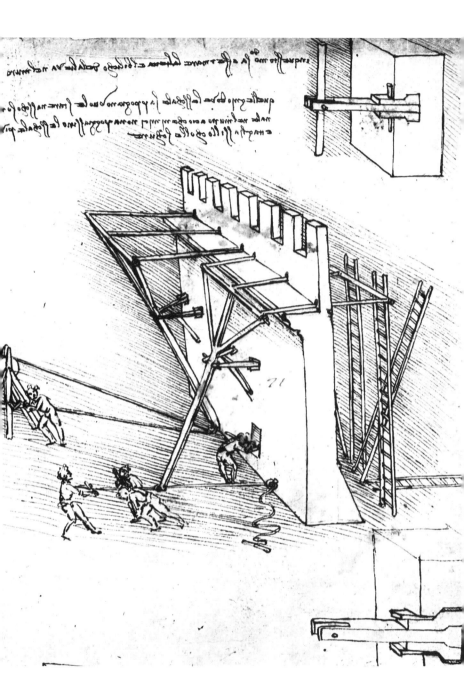

19

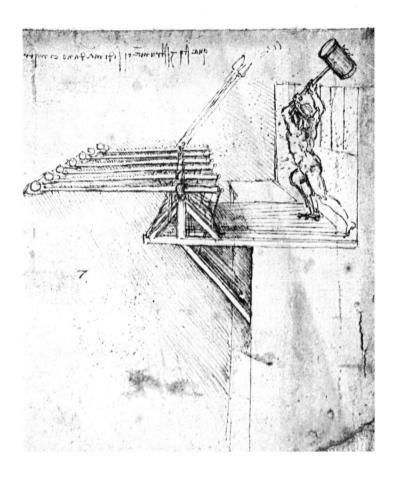

The traditional method of crushing garlic at the Sforza Palace in Milan was to give it to the hammer-man who lived on the battlements of the castle and leave him to work on it. Leonardo, finding this method both wasteful of effort and garlic devised the handy little gadget right – one squeeze with the hands and the garlic clove was crushed – and also, if you so wished, the parsley shredded. The design of what is still called in Italian kitchens, 'The Leonardo' has remained virtually unchanged to this day.

Cod. Atl. fol. 57v–a, b. (above) Cod. Atl. fol. 3v.a.

However, there is such an uproar among the tavern's clientele when Leonardo invents and serves them what today we would call the 'nouvelle cuisine' – tiny portions of exquisite little delicacies placed on exquisite little carved shapes of hard porridge and all beautifully arranged – instead of what they are accustomed to, platters piled high and indiscriminately with half a dozen different meats on top of the dreaded porridge – that Leonardo has to flee for his life; fortunately back to Verrochio's studio where he can find refuge in the Baptism of Christ painting.

Leonardo's experience in the Snails' kitchens has had considerable effect on his enquiring mind. It has shown him how primitive, and how wasteful of time and labour, the preparation of foodstuffs is in his day. And more and more from now on he is thinking up what we would call 'labour-saving gadgets' for the kitchen. He starts keeping his Note Books about now, and it is quite surprising how many of the designs in them, and which interpreters of his works have been telling us for the last four hundred years are Engines of War, Leonardo actually intended to be quite the opposite –

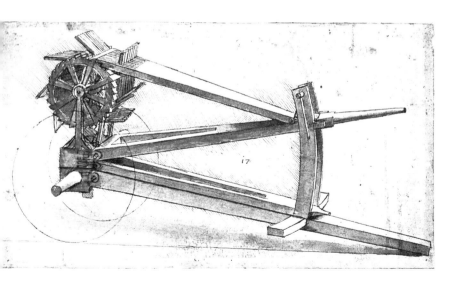

Engines of Peace, meat grinders, washing machines, mechanical nut-crackers and the like. But just now, he has to wait some time before he can turn Design into Reality. There are commissions for portraits, commissions for altar-pieces, and a reputation as a Painter to be made.

Then in the summer of 1478, following a fight between rival Florentine gangs, the famous Tavern of the Three Snails burns down. Leonardo, abandoning the most impor-tant commission he has so far received, an altarpiece for the Chapel of San Bernardo in the Palazzo Vecchio, immedi-ately proceeds with his friend Botticelli to open up a makeshift premise – mostly manufactured from old canvas-ses in Verrochio's studio – on the site, and call it Sandro and Leonardo's Sign of the Three Frogs. Leonardo paints one side of the sign hanging outside the premises, Botticelli the other.

The establishment is not a success. Florentine café society once again does not go wild over four little slithers of carrot and an anchovy – however cleverly arranged – on a platter; (and anyway, as Botticelli complains, who's going to under-stand any menu that's been written from right to left?) Verrochio's canvasses are taken down from their scaffolding and smuggled back into the Master's studio.

The ensuing three years are not good years for Leonardo. No tavern will employ him as cook or give him any job in its kitchens because of the dire effects his eccentric cookery seems to have on any clientele. He shows no inclination to go back to his altarpiece or continue with any other of his painting commissions. He just sits around Florence, dood-ling, playing the lute and inventing new knots to tie. About the most positive thing he does is to send a number of designs for battering rams and superior scaling ladders to Lorenzo de Medici, the ruler of Florence, who is just now engaged in a small war with the Pope. While Leonardo sends these as a gesture of goodwill to help in the war effort, as he accom-panies his designs with models of these machines made in marzipan and pastry, these good intentions are not fully understood by Lorenzo who simply thinks they are eccentric cakes and serves them up to his guests at dinner.

Leonardo, unthanked, unpaid, unwilling to return to the monotony of altarpieces, increasingly feels misunderstood. Still in a state of depression following his second big culinary failure, he is ready to pack his bags and leave Florence. So when Lorenzo hears that Leonardo is serious about going he gives him – partly to make amends for eating his marzipan models – a letter of introduction to Ludovico Sforza, 'Il Moro', the ruler of Milan. But when Leonardo opens it he finds no mention of his painting or cooking abilities, just that

Leonardo's foot-operated tumble drier (approximately 20 feet high and operated by six members of the kitchen staff). After he invented napkins finding ways of keeping them clean became an obsession with Leonardo.
Cod. Atl. fol. 387r. a–b.

Lorenzo is recommending him as an accomplished lute player.

In 1482 Leonardo goes with his friend the musician Atalante Migliorotti to Milan, and also with an additional letter of introduction to Il Moro, one he has written himself :

> I am without peer at making bridges, fortifications and catapults; and also many secret devices which I dare not describe on this paper. My painting and my sculpture will stand comparison with that of any other artist. I am supreme at telling riddles and tying knots. And I make cakes that are without compare.

Ludovico, when he reads Leonardo's modest self-reference, is intrigued. He grants Leonardo audience, and is so impressed by him that Leonardo leaves the Audience Chamber as Il Moro's Adviser on Fortifications and Master of the Revels and Feasting at the Sforza Court. At last, he feels, he is *Somebody*, not just a mere artist and scribbler. He is given his own servants, his own workshop, and all around him is the great Court of Milan – courtiers, advisers, soldiers of fortune, representatives of foreign powers, great scholars. At the drop of a letter his whole life has changed. This is when he starts to write the entries in his Note Books which make up Codex Romanoff.

And yet, initially, Ludovico only uses Leonardo as an after-dinner entertainer – playing his lute, singing, telling riddles, making puzzles and practical jokes, demonstrating knots to the Court. He appears totally disinterested in the designs for fortifications that Leonardo produces, and when Leonardo, realizing his Patron's preference for the more sensual things of life, resorts to making models of his proposed fortifications in sugar and quivering jellies, the same fate befalls these as did those he made in marzipan for Lorenzo de Medici. Just how many of Leonardo's designs never see the light of day because of this fate we will never know.

(*to page 29*)

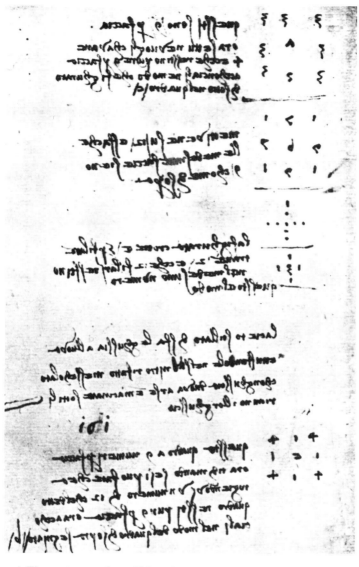

A Florentine version of Noughts and Crosses appears on this menu Leonardo was drafting for use in The Tavern of the Three Frogs at the time he and Sandro Botticelli were running it.

Cod. Atl. fol. 348r–a.

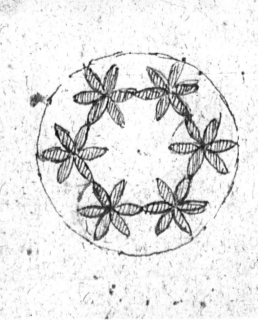

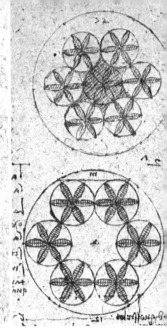

FIG. 1   FIG. 2

Leonardo based his 'nouvelle cuisine' on his disapproval of
the massive plates of cow-bones served up at table in his day,
and his preference for the attractive look of any simple veg-
etarian dish he could create as an alternative.

Early efforts such as he offered his patrons at the Tavern of
the Three Snails in Florence (as in fig. 1) were restricted to
displaying carefully arranged and identically-sized leaves of
basil stuck with calf's saliva on rounds of the local grey bread.

When patrons served this little delicacy complained it was
not a dish enough for working men Leonardo placed thin
rounds of white Bologna sausage between the bread and the
basil leaves (as in fig. 2). And when those same patrons
complained that this still did not constitute a decent meal
Leonardo simply placed many more overlapping sausage
rounds adorned with basil on even larger rounds of grey
bread (as in fig. 3). But this was still not enough to please his
customers and he narrowly missed being trampled to death
by them when they invaded his kitchen to demand more
solid fare.

Cod. Atl. fols. 89v–a, 89r–a, 88v–a.

26

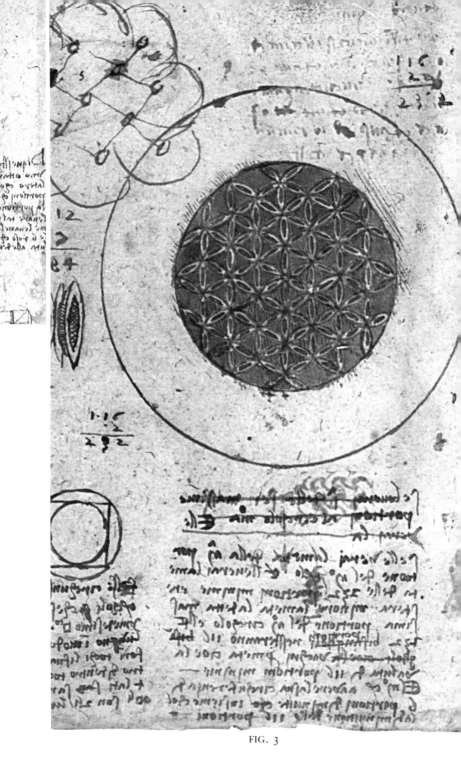

FIG. 3

ABOVE: Leonardo's design for a table
decoration in marzipan and coloured jellies.
MsB. fol. 17v.

RIGHT: Cross-section of Leonardo's
famous jelly mould.
Cod. Atl. fol. 7, v–6.

True, Leonardo does manage to occupy himself with other matters more worthy of his intellect. He reluctantly gets down to some portraits of Ladies of the Court, starting many but finishing few. He becomes heavily involved in creating a statue of Ludovico's father, a four-times life-size equestrian piece. And when there is to be a very special Feast to celebrate the wedding of a Sforza niece he takes the opportunity to propagate once again that cuisine which had met with such disasters in Florence. He takes his proposed menu for the occasion to Ludovico. Each guest, Leonardo explains to an unbelieving Ludovico, will have a platter laid before them containing:

- a rolled anchovy lying atop a slice of turnip
  carved in the likeness of a frog
- another anchovy curled round a sprout
- a carrot, beautifully carved
- the heart of an artichoke
- two half-gherkins upon the leaf of a lettuce
- the breast of a warbler
- the egg of a lapwing
- the testicle of a sheep in cream (cold)
- the leg of a frog on a dandelion leaf
- the cooked foot of a sheep, boned

As one might have surmised Ludovico tells Leonardo this is not the meal he has in mind at all. He carefully explains to Leonardo it is not the sort of Feast the Sforzas are accustomed to serve to their guests, nor the sort of Feast that Sforza guests are going to be prepared to travel hundreds of miles to sample at the end of their arduous journeying. And from the Sforza accounting books we know what Ludovico ordered Leonardo to supply instead:

- 600 Pigs-brain sausages from Bologna
- 300 Zampone (stuffed pigs legs) from Modena
- 1200 round pies from Ferrara
- 200 of calves, capons and geese
- 60 of peacocks, swans and heron

Some of Leonardo's designs for folding of table napkins. Others were more elaborate and the napkins were made in the shapes of birds, flowers and palaces.
Cod. Atl. fol. 167r. a–b.

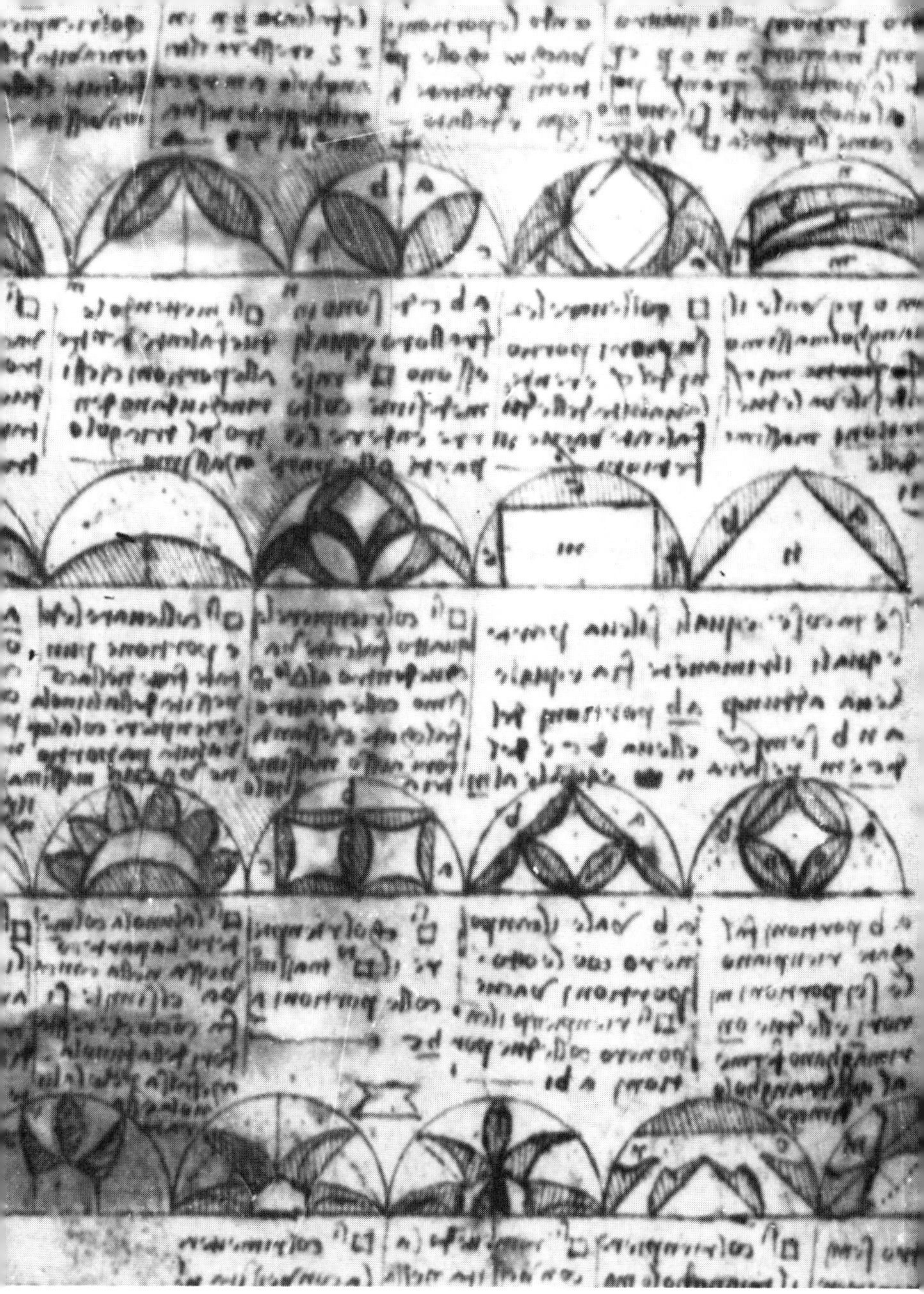

- marzipan from Siena
- cheese from Gorgonzola that must bear
  the stamp of the Cheesemongers Guild
- the mince of Monza
- 2000 oysters of Venice
- macaroni from Genoa
- enough sturgeon
- truffles
- and mashed turnips

Similar ingredients are to be the order of the day at all the Feasts that Leonardo subsequently has to organize for Ludovico.

But at least Ludovico has recognized Leonardo's interest – however eccentric – in food and shortly afterwards he asks Leonardo to redesign the kitchens of the Castello, the great Sforza Palace in the middle of Milan.

From that moment on, and for the ensuing half year, Ludovico and the hundreds who comprise his Court and live in the Palace, don't know what's hit them.

Leonardo immediately compiles a list of what he considers are the main requirements of a kitchen:

Firstly, [one needs] a constant source of fire. Then a constant supply of water that boils. Then a floor that is forever clean. Then Devices for Cleaning, Grinding, Slicing, Peeling and Cutting. Then a Device for keeping Stinks and Stenches away from the kitchen and ennobling it with a Sweet and Smokeless atmosphere. And then Musick, for men work better and more happily where there is Musick. And finally a Device for eliminating frogs from the barrels of drinking water.

And then Leonardo sits down in his huge workshop in the Corte Vecchio (now Palazzo Reale) where normally scenery for the Castello entertainments is made, and invents. (We know all this from Matteo Bandelli who has the odd appointment of Court Novelist.) Leonardo starts with absolute basics. Will a log of one particular shape and length burn better and provide more heat than any other, he asks himself.

For days he studies fires burning different logs, timing how long each takes to burn, measuring how much heat it gives off. But in the end he concludes it's quantity of any shaped logs that matters, and invents a conveyor belt whereby logs cut by a circular saw positioned outside the kitchen are delivered straight to the side of the fires – thus he declares, eliminating the need for the logman in the kitchen (though ignoring the four other men and eight horses operating and feeding his circular saw outside).

He also designs an Automatic Roaster which is intended to release one member of the kitchen staff from having to spend all day turning a spit over the fire. Set in the chimney over the fire, the propeller is turned by the upward draft of hot air and is itself attached to gears which turn the spit. 'The roast will turn slow or fast depending on whether the fire is small or strong,' Leonardo has written beneath his design for it (in Codex Atlanticus, and there is also a working model of it on display at the Museo della Scienza e della Tecnica in Milan). Though Leonardo doesn't specify what the kitchen hand freed from spit-turning should now do with his time.

For his 'constant supply of water that boils' Leonardo devises a charcoal-operated geyser – a long series of coiled metal tubes constantly being refilled and lying in the ashes of the fire. He has some doubts as to whether it is as efficient as the old crone who normally keeps a pot boiling over the fire, but expresses the belief (to Matteo Bandelli) that his design is more in keeping with the enlightened age he lives in.

The 'floor that is forever clean' is produced by two oxen harnessed to a revolving brush one and a half meters in diameter and two and a half meters wide with a scoop behind it to collect what it picks up. It takes up more room than the old man with the broom who performed the task previously but is obviously more effective than he.

Leonardo plans to power his 'Devices for Cleaning, Grinding, and etc' partly from a great water-wheel he wants to construct at one end of his kitchen, and partly by horse-power. His most massive device, the Cow Grinder (his

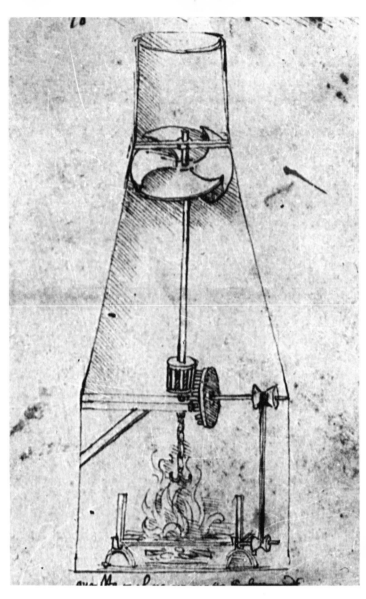

Leonardo's design for an Automatic Roaster – the fan, or propeller, in the chimney is turned by hot air from the fire and powers the split below.
Cod. Atl. fol. 5v.

designs for which appear both in the Vatican Library and in the Queen of England's collection at Windsor Castle – although it has been suggested that one might be by a pupil) appears to need a small army of men to work it – with an equal number of horses – and it apparently has a whole series of attachments, much like the blending machines of to-day, for grinding pigs and smaller animals.

And there is also amongst Leonardo's Devices a wind-powered bread-slicing machine which cuts, then threads, pieces of bread together on long reeds. It is twice as large as the existing bakery attached to the old kitchens at the Castello, and Leonardo notes that the Armoury adjacent to the

Leonardo's 'blender-blade' attachment designed to be worked by cogs and hand-crank, and to replace the multipurpose pestle and mortar of the time. Although in his lifetime Leonardo had difficulty finding anything to which he could attach it, Melzi records that thirty years after his death a close variation of it was in use at the main sausage factory of Milan.

MsB. fol. 83v.

premises will have to be taken over when the work of reconstruction starts. He also informs Ludovico that his kitchen expansion programme will require nearly one half of the Great Hall of the Castello, the adjacent stables, and the six rooms that Ludovico's mother inhabits and which Leonardo needs as a combined vegetable store and slaughterhouse.

For the music in his kitchens Leonardo plans to use the hand-cranked mechanical drums he has already invented and had made, accompanied by three musicians playing an instrument he now plans to invent and which he describes as a mouth-organ.

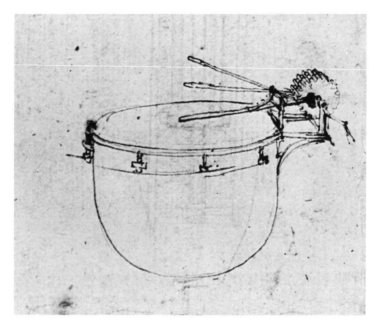

Leonardo's design for a semi-mechanical drum (the beaters turned by a cog-wheel operated by a hand-crank) which was one of the musical instruments intended to accompany work in the new kitchens he designed for Ludovico Sforza in Castello Sforza.
Cod. Atl. 355r–c.

His 'Device for keeping Stinks and Stenches away' turns out to be no more than some great bellows attached to the ceilings and operated by the upward action of a series of hammers attached to a horse-propelled crank-shaft.

While his 'Device for eliminating Frogs from barrels of drinking water' is a simple spring trap which, when any frog hops on, causes a series of hammer blows to be delivered to its head until, presumably, the frog loses consciousness and so is in no state to jump into the drinking water.

And there is one other revolutionary feature he plans for his kitchen – which he has not referred to in his original memorandum – which is an ingenious sprinkler system ready to douse everything – if it works to plan – in the event of fire.

So all this is what Leonardo invents as the contents of his new kitchen – which is not to say that it is all going to work perfectly, or indeed work at all. Leonardo is always much stronger on Theory than Practice.

So then work starts on the project in earnest. Old walls come down and new walls go up. The alterations to the Great Hall that Leonardo demands make the place impossible to eat in and Ludovico and his Court, anyway unable to get any service because the old kitchens are out of action, have to eat out at the tables of friends or retire to Ludovico's country estate at Vigevano.

And just when the building work is at its most hectic Leonardo gets offered one of the great opportunities of his painting life. The Confraternity of the Immaculate Conception, a sort of religious Mafia of Milan to whose offer nobody ever says No, have had a great gilt frame made for the altarpiece of the church of San Frenesco Grande, and they want Leonardo to execute the centre portion of it. Leonardo, who does not want to get out his brushes at what he considers such a vital moment in his culinary career, tries to stall the powerful Confraternity by saying he thinks he's got just the thing for them, something he's brought in his baggage from

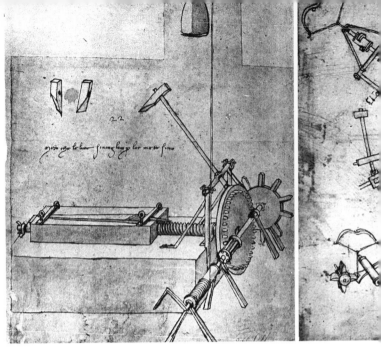

Leonardo's 'Device for Eliminating frogs from Drinking Water'. When the frog hopped onto the baited trap a hammer would deliver a blow to its head and continue delivering such blows until the frog became unconscious. (Multiple versions of the same shown.)
Cod. Atl. fols. 6, 7. (left) Cod. Atl. 217a. (right)

Florence and which has been lying around ever since, a Virgin of the Rocks. The Confraternity look at it but point out it's the wrong size for their frame; but in the end, seeing in what a hassle Leonardo finds himself, they relent and agree that, if it will help, he can do them a slightly different size copy* of it for their church – which is what, in the midst of his kitchen-fitting Leonardo does – or rather, starts to do.

*Leonardo's original Virgin of the Rocks is in the Louvre in Paris. The version he eventually completed for the Confraternity is in the National Gallery, London.

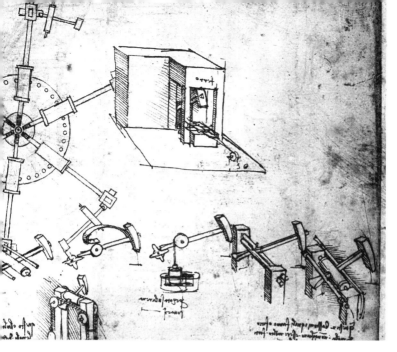

Soon the pressures of having at the same time to think up what foods are going to be served on his 'opening night' are too many for him to be able to concentrate on the painting, and it's put away – like so many of his other works – for 'another day', and he gets down to his menus. He knows he's not going to get away with a few pretty carrots and that it's got to be traditional Milanese foods so he sits down to devise great pies and taste endless sauces, he calls in the finest sausage-makers, hires the best carvers, and finally the day comes when he announces that his new kitchens are ready to dispense food. At the eleventh hour, just to feel true to himself and his food beliefs, he's requested that the meal start with everyone being served a large beet carved in the likeness of Ludovico's very recognizable face and resting on two lettuce leaves. There's been near-insurrection in the kitchens because of the request, the cooks complaining they do not normally expect to have to carve as well as cook vegetables, and Leonardo has had to bring in all the artists and sculptors of Milan to perform the task. So their presence

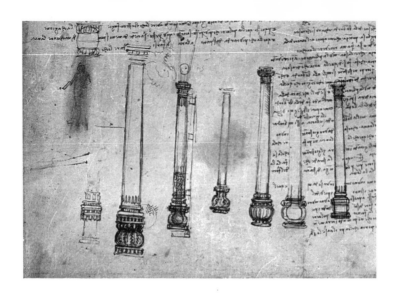

Leonardo: Designs for pepper mills.
Cod. Atl. fol. 28v–a.

is adding to the existing chaos in the kitchens – Leonardo's sprinkler system has mysteriously come on and can't be quelled, and two of the cooks have demanded suits of armour on account of the hazards of working with uncontrollable machinery.

Meanwhile Ludovico, his guests and the Court have taken their places at table in the much-diminished Great Hall of the Castello. After an hour of not receiving any food, just listening to the most amazing series of screams, explosions, grindings and crankings of machinery coming from the kitchens, Ludovico and some companions go to investigate.

In the monthly report he returns to the Signoria of Florence, Sabba da Castiglione di Pietro Alemanni, the Florentine Ambassador to the Sforza Court, and who is amongst this company, describes the scene they come across:

Master Leonardo's kitchen is a bedlam. Lord Ludovico has told me that the effort of the last months had been to economize upon human labour, but now, instead of the twenty cooks the kitchens did once employ, there are closer to two

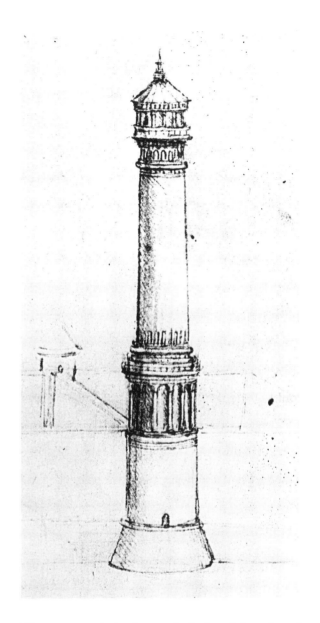

The pepper-grinder Leonardo designed, based on the
great Spezia lighthouse, to be made in vine-wood
for Ludovico Sforza.
MsB. fol. 23v.

hundred persons milling in the area, and none that I could see cooking but all attending to the great devices that crowded up the floors and walls, and none of which seemed behaving in any manner useful or for which it was created.

At one end of the premise a great water-wheel, driven by a raging waterfall over it, spewed and spattered forth its waters over all who passed beneath, and made the floor a lake. Giant bellows, each [twelve foot] long were suspended from the ceilings, hissing and roaring with intent to clear the fire smoke, but all they did accomplish was to fan the flames to the detriment of all who needed to negotiate by the fires – so fierce the wandering flames that a constant stream of men

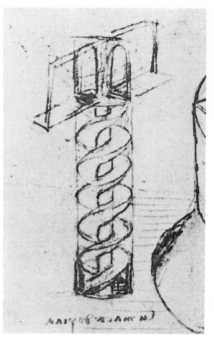

Leonardo's design for a left-handed corkscrew. It was only after inventing it that he set to work to find out how to insert corks into bottles – which in his time, if used at all, were normally sealed with wax.
Ms B. fol. 69r.

42

Leonardo's Giant Cow Grinder. One of the designs similar to those in the Windsor Collection, England, copied by Leonardo's pupil Francesco Melzi from his Master's original, which was in the Royal Palace, Turin, and has now been moved to Biblioteca Trivulziana, Milan.
William Thomson Collection.

with buckets was employed in trying to quell them, even though other waters spouted forth on all from every corner of the ceilings.

And throughout this stricken area wandered horses and oxen, some going round and round to turn an apparatus the function of which seemed to be no more than to go around and round, the others dragging Master Leonardo's floor-cleaning devices – performing their tasks valiantly, but also followed by another great army of men to clean the horses' messes.

Elsewhere I saw the great Cow-grinder broken down with half a cow still stuck out of it, and men with levers essaying to move it out. And elsewhere yet Master Leonardo's continuous Log and Firewood Device disgorging its supply into the room and could not be stopped – so that instead of two men bringing logs in for the fires as used to be, now ten did have to be employed to take them out.

The screams we had been hearing we now realized were from the poor wretches being burned or drowned or smothered, and the explosions from the gunpowders Master Leonardo did insist to use to light his smouldering fires, and as if this was not enough noise it was still combined with the music from his drums which pounded out – though those who played his mouth-organs I think were drowned.

As I did describe before, Master Leonardo's kitchen was a Bedlam, which I do not think did please Lord Ludovico.

And when, eventually, Ludovico and his party, including the Florentine Ambassador, depart from this Bedlam, they are joined in the Great Hall by a very contrite Leonardo offering them a bowl of carved beet and his apologies. Ludovico, very aware of Leonardo's genius, but desperate to divert him from further outbursts of it in this part of his Palace, congratulates Leonardo on the vision of his scheme and suggests he should take a rest in the country immediately, and perhaps paint a portrait of Ludovico's current mistress Cecilia Gallerani (the famous 'Lady with an Ermine' in the Czartoryski Museum at Cracow).

For the next few years there is comparative quiet at the Castello while Leonardo is reluctantly painting the Ladies of the Sforza Court, prevaricating over altarpieces, producing his models for bridges and forts in marzipan, sugar and quivering jelly – at all costs being encouraged in occupations which keep him as far as possible away from the kitchens. He gets as far as creating what everyone refers to as 'The Great Horse' – the equestrian statue of Ludovico's father, in clay (but not further as Ludovico claims he cannot afford the amount of bronze in which it needs to be cast). He invents, and has made a giant watercress cutter. But at its demonstration in the watercress fields outside the Sforza Palace it runs out of hand and kills six members of the kitchen staff and three gardeners. (Subsequently Ludovico uses it with great effect against French invading troops.)

Leonardo's greatest relief during this time is when he is permitted to create pageants and masques – as those he designs in 1490 to commemorate the wedding of Ludovico's nephew Duke Gian Galeazzo to Isabella of Aragon, granddaughter of the King of Naples. Leonardo turns the whole vast courtyard of the Palace into a fairyland jungle, with many of the servants dressed as wild beasts (there are many of his costume designs for these in the Royal Collection at Windsor in England) and many in bird costumes flying through the air on an intricate series of invisible wires he has devised. While in between courses at the Wedding Feast (which he has not been allowed to cater for) he arranges for fantastically-dressed tumblers, fire-eaters, midgets and belly-dancers to parade across the tables. And after the meal, during the performance of the Court Poet Bernardo Bellincioni's 'Paradiso' (the original libretto of which still exists in Milan) Leonardo contrives the Planets spinning through the sky, a twenty-foot high waterfall pouring out of the sky, and an elephant disappearing into thin air.

The sumptuousness of this Pageant he plans to exceed two years later when he makes the arrangements for Ludovico's marriage to Beatrice D'Este. The whole celebration he plans to take place *inside* a cake – a 200-foot long replica of the Sforza Palace constructed in the Palace court-yard of pre-

cast cake – mostly blocks of porridge reinforced with nuts and raisins, and covered in multi-coloured marzipans. The wedding guests will walk through doors made of cake, will sit on stools made of cake at tables made of cake from which – inevitably – they will eat cake.

The one factor that Leonardo does not allow for is the structure's attraction to the birds and rats of Milan. The night before the Wedding Feast they come from all over the surrounding countryside in their hundreds of thousands. Ludovico's men spend all night long fighting a pitched battle with them, but by dawn there is such a scene of desolation, the whole court-yard a shambles of fallen cake-work, men wading waist-high in cake-crumbs to clear away dead rats, that it becomes clear this Marriage Feast must find a new venue – which it does, on the plain outside the Palace.

Once again Ludovico behaves very graciously toward Leonardo. Perhaps it is the influence of his new wife, for Leonardo has painted Beatrice well, and she has formed quite an attraction toward him because of the riddles with which he has plied her while she sat for him. In the event, Ludovico simply suggests to Leonardo that once again his many talents might well be appreciated outside the Palace for a while and recommends him to visit the Prior of Santa Maria delle Grazie down the road who is looking for an artist to paint a blank wall in the Priory's refectory.

The work that Leonardo is eventually to execute on this wall in his Last Supper. It is going to take up three years of his life – three years not so much working on it as prevaricating about it. It is apt that the Prior gives Leonardo as the

LEFT : Leonardo abhorred wasted human effort. The primitive ways of cracking nuts as practised in Florence for hundreds of years, and which he depicts in his picture (above) tying the walnut to the end of a whip and thrashing it against the ground; attacking it with a sledge-hammer – he tried to replace with the simple spring press (below) which could be easily operated by three horses revolving round it.
William Thomson Collection.

47

subject matter for what is to become his greatest painting what is Leonardo's own favourite subject: food. And from the very start, as he confides to his friend Matteo Bandelli the novelist, he approaches the wall he is to paint with the express aim of making what he puts on it a total justification of both his past and present interest in food – a fact which must be a little disillusioning to those who in the past have only been prepared to consider the painting's more lofty and spiritual theme – which, to Leonardo was only incidental.

Matteo Bandelli tells us that during the first year of his commission all Leonardo did was to walk every now and then from the Castello to the refectory at Santa Maria delle Grazie, and there just stare for hours on end at the wall he was to paint.

Then during the latter part of 1495 he requests the Prior to provide him with a long table in the otherwise empty room, and also with foodstuffs and wines on this table which every day now Leonardo visits with his pupils and arranges and re-arranges before he sketches them.

The Prior, towards Easter 1496, writes to Ludovico in bafflement at this behaviour of Leonardo's:

> My Lord, it over twelve months since you despatched Master Leonardo to perform this commission and in all that time not one mark has he made upon our wall. And in that time, My Lord, the cellars of the Priory show vast depletion and now are nearly dry, for Master Leonardo insists all wines be tried until the right one for his masterpiece arrives – he will not have it other. And all this time my Friars go hungry for Master Leonardo puts our kitchens to his use both day and night concocting what he claims are foods he needs upon his table – but never to his total satisfaction – and then two times a day he has his followers and servants sit down to eat them all. My Lord, I urge you hasten Master Leonardo in performance of his work, for now his presence, and of his band as well, does threaten us with penury.

Raymond Perault, Bishop of Gurk, visited Leonardo at

the Priory some nine months later in January 1497. He described the experience – confirming what the Prior had written to Ludovico – in a letter to his superiors in Innsbruck:

> Master Leonardo has drawn a cartoon of some pillars and the outline of a table on his wall and below it built a platform with one long table in it; and to this table do his several helpers – who I conjectured would be employed in mixing colours – brings foods and jugs of wine which Master Leonardo looks at and re-arranges before he makes a drawing of – and then he bids all eat and drink. And this the Prior so told me has been how it was since commencement of the exercise, Master Leonardo showing interest only for the contents of his table and still yet none (that's obvious) for the persons seated at it.

Two years and nine months does seem a long time and then – and despite all the hundreds of sketches Leonardo made of different foodstuffs, from boiled eggs with carrot slices, to leg of coot with marrow flowers – then in the end come up with bread rolls, mashed turnips and slices of eel, but that, according to Matteo Bandelli, is the combination of foods that Leonardo finally arrived at to depict in his Supper after that period of time. Perhaps the key to the greatness of the painting is this simplicity and economy of foodstuffs that Leonardo chose. At any rate, after he had made his decision, after he had filled them in on the table in his painting, he then spent the final three months of his work on the whole in depicting the diners – note also, that after all the wines Leonardo tasted, the diners end up with just seven almost empty glasses between them, which could have contained a red wine.

And so Leonardo came to an end of his labours on the wall of Santa Maria delle Grazie. But such was the poor way his helpers had primed the wall, even as Leonardo was finishing the figures the foods were starting to peel off the wall. When King Louis XII of France saw the wall two years later such was its condition that his only comment was 'It must be very, very old.' And when they then told him it was the work of Leonardo he refused to believe it.

Leonardo's fanatical interest in food is never so intense again after he completes his Last Supper. It is as though in those slices of eel, mashed turnips and bread rolls he has depicted in his painting he has made his ultimate statement about food, and he can now, at any rate for the time being, concern himself with other matters.

But still, and in despite of his increasing fame, there are financial problems. During 1495 he had had to address a note to Ludovico to complain of arrears of salary: 'My Lord, I have kept six mouths for thirty-six months and have had but fifty ducats, and hear that all this time you have been regularly paying such unworthies as potters, bell-ringers, and even *bombardiers*.'

This is the real reason Leonardo has been bringing his

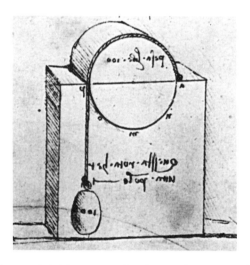

Leonardo's 'Apparatus for Suspending an Egg'.
Cod. Atl. fol. 363 v.c.

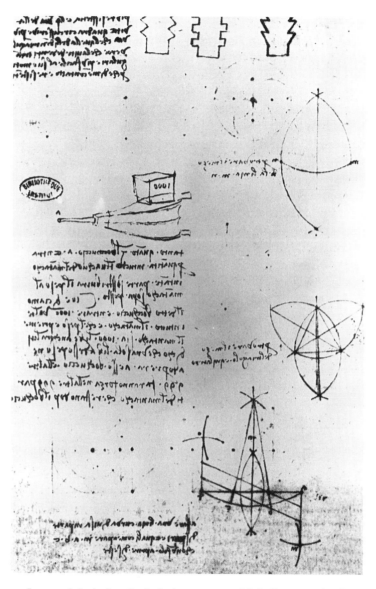

Leonardo's design for inflating an egg with bellows so that it
can be split into three equal halves.
MsA. fol. 15v.

followers and servants down to the Priory to eat every day. And a little later, according to Matteo Bandelli, reports are circulating that Leonardo, to make some money for his staff's upkeep, is running a public restaurant actually inside the Castello, using the now abandoned kitchen wing for the venture. If Ludovico knows of this he is perhaps turning a blind eye to it, knowing that it is his own neglect of Leonardo's upkeep that is to blame. But Ludovico now considers he must save all money to put into arms against the threatened French invasion of Milan that he foresees. Regarding this, he has a request to make of Leonardo; although before he makes it, and also perhaps to make some small amend for his lack of financial support, he makes a gift to Leonardo of a small vineyard on the outskirts of Milan. (Leonardo immediately hands it over to Giovanni Battista, a relative of his cook, with instructions to make it as productive as possible as quickly as possible.) But the request that Ludovico then makes is that Leonardo should do a survey of the fortresses around Milan and work out what changes might be made to them (and for these he gives Leonardo a free hand) in the light of this threatened French invasion.

Leonardo visits the fortresses. Either because he's still annoyed with Ludovico about money, or perhaps because he foresees the days of peace when a chain of restaurants – as opposed to forts – can serve up his nouvelle cuisine to travellers and visiting invaders, he orders that all the ammunition chambers of the fortresses be cleared and fitted out as kitchens. Consequently when Louis XII of France finally does invade Milan the following year the forts all fall easily to him – the Milanese soldiery in them anyway all drunk on the wine from Leonardo's vineyard that he insists their commanders purchase. Almost the only French casualties in this campaign are caused by Ludovico putting Leonardo's

RIGHT : Leonardo's design for a Wind-up Egg Slicer. Cod. Atl. fol. 56v.a.

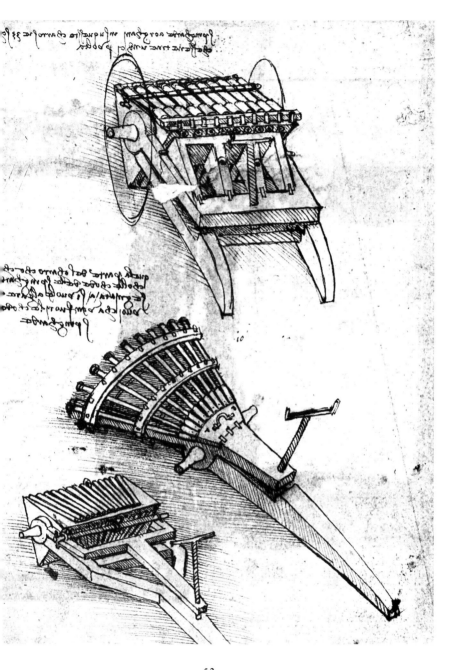

53

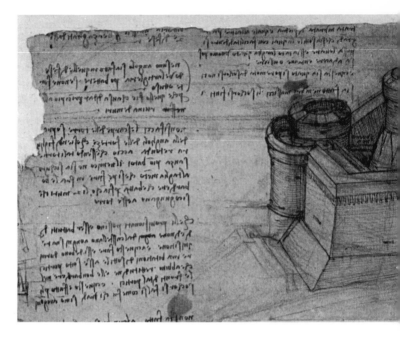

water-cress cutter into action against them. Ludovico is taken prisoner, and Leonardo, rather than suffer the indignities of French cooking under a French occupation of the Castello, leaves Milan with his friend Luca Pacioli and goes off on a gastronomic tour of Venice.

The ensuing sixteen years (1500–1516) are unsettled years for Leonardo. He spends the first six months in Florence at the friary of the Annunziata, accepting lodging for himself and his pupils in return for a double ancona he says he will paint for the friars. At the end of six months all he's accomplished is the mixing of the varnish for the finished picture which he hasn't even commenced. He takes service under the Borgias advising them on fortifications. He returns to Florence to paint – at his own instigation – Mona Lisa, the wife of the merchant Francesco Giacondo. No one understands why the task takes him a whole year and unfortunately there is a complete lack of facts which offer any explanation. Then he and MichelAngelo are commissioned

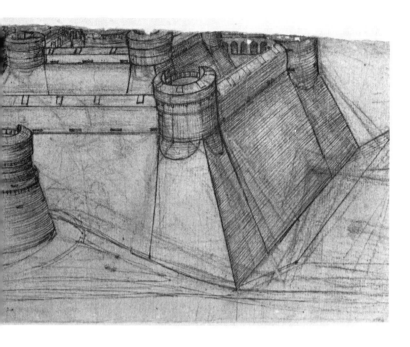

Leonardo's very military design for an eight-burner stove such as he planned to instal in his proposed chain of fortified restaurants in Lombardy.
Col. Atl. fol. 41v–b.

by the Signoria of Florence each to paint their version of the Battle of Anghiani on walls of the Council Chamber. MichelAngelo gets on with his, while Leonardo spends his whole time devising a collapsible scaffolding from which he will paint his, and paints nothing at all. He goes back to Milan to work for King Louis of France. In 1509 we learn that Leonardo has under his 'command' a band of artists who during Louis' campaign against Venice have to substitute the French fleur-de-lys for the Venetian Lion of St Mark with every fresh conquest that Louis makes. Then the King puts him on to designing canals. And somewhere along the line, it's not quite clear when, or where, he comes up with one of his most far-reaching gastronomic discoveries. Leonardo invents spaghetti.

Leonardo invents spaghetti. That is really an over-simplification. Marco Polo had brought back from China over 200 years earlier something which *looked* like spaghetti (but was really noodles) but what he hadn't told people was that you *ate* the stuff, and anyway most people who had any of it just left it lying around as a table decoration. And then

An early design of Leonardo's for converting lasagne to spaghetti. The lasagne of those days being a thick very tough substance, Leonardo thought that rather than dampen it and roll it out into something finer and thinner, he would stretch it so. But when he had his machine made his theory proved totally impractical, the lasagne snapping the moment it came under any tension.
Cod. Atl. fol. 51r.

we have to remember that pasta had existed in Italy, especially in Naples and the South, since time immemorial. Mostly it was quite thick and very wide, like a large, heavy layer of lasagne. What Leonardo does is to change its shape by devising a machine which turns it into long thin string-like pieces which, when cut up and placed in the boiling pot, becomes spaghetti – or as Leonardo refers to it *spago mangiabile* (edible twine). However, it doesn't catch on.* People regard it and just think what a mess it looks, and ask themselves how they can be expected to eat it with a knife. Which is what then prompts Leonardo to invent the three-pronged fork – even in large households there is only one fork in these days, a large two-pronged affair which is for kitchen use only. But Leonardo's *spago mangiabile* still doesn't catch on as not enough people know he's invented this device to make it edible. However, Leonardo has such faith in his new foodstuff that the machine with which he makes it, encased in a voluminous black box, never leaves his side for the rest of his life.

Leonardo in 1516 is tired of failure, and weary of the unsettled life he has been leading. When the young King Henry, who has succeeded Louis XII of France, and who is anxious to establish a reputation as a patron of the arts, and who has in the brief time he has known Leonardo become a great devotee of his *spago mangiabile*, offers him a considerable income, a small Palace to live in (and, what really counts to Leonardo, his own kitchen to work in). Leonardo, without any serious Patron left in Italy now, readily accepts, and joins the French King's retinue back to Amboise in the Loire valley. He takes with him Francesco Melzi, his most faithful

There is indeed one school of thought which claims that spaghetti as such didn't catch on in Italy until after the Americans introduced it in tins and with tomato sauce and meatballs in 1945, Leonardo did not of course have the advantage of tomatoes which did not reach Europe – from Mexico – until the late sixteenth century and even then, to begin with, were used in their green form and only as decorations on clothing and hats.

Leonardo's spaghetti-winder.
Cod. Atl. 2v.a.

Leonardo's device for testing the tensile strength of spaghetti.
Cod. Atl. 2v.b.

pupil, and his old cook Battista de Villanis. They travel by muleback over the Alps, one mule carrying all Leonardo's Note Books, his Mona Lisa and St John paintings, and the vital black box. And they finally arrive at the manor house of Cloux (now Clos-Luce) beside Francis' great chateau on the banks of the Loire at Amboise. Here Leonardo is to spend his last three years. He has planned, not to paint, not to write further Notes, but just to put in order his existing Note Books and make one great encyclopaedia out of their contents. It doesn't work out this way however. The reason being that King Francis is really a closet cook and uses Leonardo as a cover for his illicit visits to a kitchen. A tunnel is built between Francis's great Palace and Leonardo's small manor to expedite the King's visits, and day after day he and Leonardo spend hours experimenting in the simple stone kitchen at Cloux. Leonardo finally is leading the life he has always wanted.

To aid the King and he in their endeavours there is a plentiful supply of birds and game in the area, there are any amount of fish to be caught in the Loire or sent from Bordeaux, and Leonardo personally supervises the planting of a vegetable garden that you can still see stocked with similar vegetables to-day.

Time and again Francis requests Leonardo to release the contents of his black box so that it can be copied and Francis can make spaghetti the national dish of France, but for some unexplained reason Leonardo is reluctant to part with it. Perhaps he sees it, as he once saw his Last Supper, as his supreme gift to the world and he doesn't want others to get hold of it and misuse it. He gives Francis his Mona Lisa, he gives Francis his St John, but what is really valuable to Leonardo is his device in the box and he has decided it stays with him to death.

In another way Leonardo has to disappoint Francis too. Francis keeps bringing a favourite of his, one Babou de la Bourdaisiere, to Cloux to be painted by Leonardo, and

Leonardo keeps making up excuses as to why he can't paint the lady – reasonable excuses, like his arthritis in the hands which is troubling him much now. But Francis persists, and in the end Leonardo gets his pupil Melzi to paint Babou as Clementine and every now and then when Francis is present adds a brush stroke himself.

But basically the two men are at Cloux to cook and eat. It might seem strange that Leonardo isn't making notes of their experiments and the resultant dishes, but perhaps he is, and perhaps one day like so many others of his lost writings they are going to turn up. We have waited a long time to read all the notes he made on cooking while in Ludovico's service, we can wait a little longer for the notes of his collaboration with the French King.

Leonardo enjoys three years of this life before he dies in 1519. It may not be true, as Vasari writes in his *Lives of the Painters*, and as any number of very sentimental paintings by others show, that Leonardo dies cradled in the arms of King Francis. But it's possible.

Leonardo, in his will, leaves half of his vineyard outside Milan to Battista his cook, half to Salai the young boy who became his servant in 1490, and his pupil Melzi gets all the Note Books and personal effects. When Melzi opens the Black Box it is empty, and we never hear another word as to what might have happened to its contents.

THE CODEX ROMANOFF
❖❖❖❖❖ OF ❖❖❖❖❖
LEONARDO DA VINCI

❖ INTRODUCTORY NOTE ❖

The cookery notes that Leonardo wrote down and which have been compiled to make the Codex Romanoff are far from comprehensive of the foods and dishes available in his time. He seems to have written down quite randomly just the things that interested him. His recipes are other people's, not of his own devising – except when he goes back to propagating the totally lost cause of his 'nouvelle cuisine'. Though in his observations on cookery and eating, and especially in the changes he plans for kitchens, he is more inventive.

Food in Milan – indeed food all over Italy – during the years that Leonardo wrote these entries in his Note Books (most of them from between 1481 and 1500) can only be described as quite horrible. The days of larks' tongues, of scrambled ostrich eggs, of pigs stuffed with black pudding and live thrushes, the days of the gluttony of Ancient Rome are long over. Food is now Gothic – meaning as introduced into Italy by the Goths. The rich eat profusions of meats and birds, the poor *polenta*, or porridge, or sometimes coarse soups and gruels. Nearly everything is highly spiced – or rather, heavily herbed (including the porridge). Most green and root vegetables exist – but not the potato, not the tomato or any of the others which are discovered in the New World but not put to general use in Europe before the seventeenth century. There is salt, pepper and spices, there are cheeses, there is bread (though white is a great rarity), the sweetener is honey as it has always been, not sugar (though there is sugar-cane growing in Sicily). Wine is nearly always mixed with water or honey or both. And drinking water can be rare, obtained only from aqueducts or water carriers.

Brandy is a medicine for the plague-ridden, distilled and distributed by the apothecaries. There is no tea, coffee or chocolate. The commonest kitchen instruments are the pestle and mortar – nearly all meat, fish and poultry is pounded to the consistency of a fine paté, put through a sieve then mixed with honey and rice (to make it go further). Food is served on trenchers – flat bread which is afterwards eaten, or in some richer households given to the dogs or the poor. The poor eat once a day, at midday. The rich have a small meal between 9 and 10 am and their main meal in the early evening. But on the bright side, the sturgeon being the most common fish in the Mediterranean, the poor never lack for caviare.

Not unnaturally, bearing in mind Leonardo's position when he wrote these entries – as Master of the Revels and Feasting at the Court of the Sforzas – what he notes down is from the vantage point of a very rich household indeed. So not all that surprisingly, caviare being such a 'common' dish, it doesn't crop up at all in his recipes. It's even beneath porridge in his estimation.

The main persons referred to by Leonardo in the following pages are:

'*My Lord Lodovico*': Ludovico Sforza, 'Il Moro', the ruler of Milan, Leonardo's patron from 1481–1499, subsequently, on the death of his ineffectual younger brother Giancarlo in 1495, Duke of Milan.
'*My Lady Beatrice*': Beatrice D'Este who became Ludovico's wife in 1493.
Salai, Leonardo's pupil/servant from 1490 on (real name Gian Giacomo Caprotti di Oreno).
Battista, Leonardo's cook.

(Other persons referred to by Leonardo are explained in footnotes.)

An illustration from the Cook Book of Bartolomeo Scappi, the 'secret' cook book of Pope Pius V, depicts the way that a meal was served at the Sforza court in Milan.

67

On the Table Manners of
My Lord Lodovico and
his Table Guests

My Lord Lodovico's habit of tethering beribboned rabbits to the chairs of his table guests, that they may wipe their grease-ridden hands upon the beasts' backs I find unseemly for the day and age we live in. Also, when the beasts are collected after the meal and taken to the laundry-room, their stink pervades the other linens with which they are washed.

Neither do I care for My Lord's habit of wiping his knife upon his neighbour's skirts. Whyfor can he not, like the other members of his Court, wipe it upon the tablecloth which is so provided ?

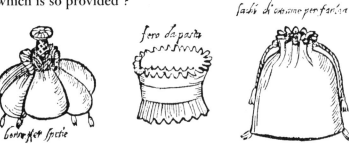

On the Correct Manner
to Choose a Cheese

To detect whether the large cheeses of Parma and the Romagna may be hollow – for there are unscrupulous cheese-sellers in these areas who will offer you such – always, before purchasing, put your ear to its side and tap it with your hammer, listening intently to detect any sounds of hollowness. Then, if you are satisfied it is solid throughout, you may purchase it. This was taught me by Agnolo di Polo who was a sculptor and noted cheese-fancier in the workshop of the great Verocchio.

sifa lauoreri de latte

neueue si fa

Luochi freschi doue fa lauoreri de latte

latte mele si fa

69

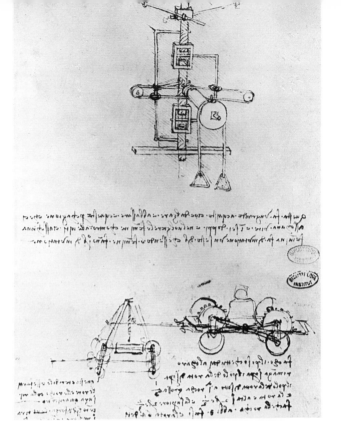

ABOVE: Leonardo's Revolving Napkin Drier driven by a man seated in stirrups. Also mobile versions of the same. MsB. fol. 77r.

BELOW: Another of Leonardo's revolving napkin driers, this one to be operated by bees, he wrote. Cod. Atl. fol. 57r–6.

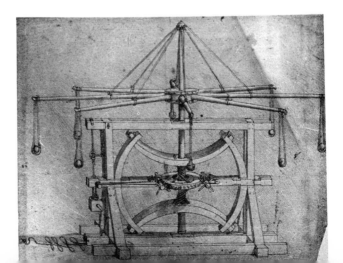

On an Alternative to
Filthy Tablecloths

Upon inspection of My Lord Lodovico's tablecloths once his guests have departed the dining hall I find myself surveying a scene of such utter mess and depravation – resembling nothing so much as the aftermath of a battlefield – that I now consider it my priority, before any Horse or Altarpiece, to discover an alternative.

I have one already. I have in mind that everyone at table should be given their own cloth which, after soiling with their filthy hands and knives, they can then fold over so as not to desecrate the appearance of the table with their filths. But what should I call these cloths ? And how should I present them ?*

*Leonardo himself makes no further mention in words of his proposal for a napkin (though see his designs for different models of it in the illustration on p. 30–31), but Pietro Alemanni, the Florentine Ambassador to Milan, refers to it in one of his reports (dated July 1491) back to the Signoria at Florence (Annali di Firenze Vol XIV pp 314–5).

'As Your Lordships have required me to furnish Yourselves with further details of Master Leonardo's career at Lord Lodovico's Court I do so. He has of late been neglecting his Sculptures and Geometry and been applying himself to the problems of Lord Lodovico's tablecloth, the filth on which – he confides to me – has caused him much distress. And this last eve he produced at table his solution to it and which was an individual cloth placed on the table in front of each guest and which he was meant to sully rather than the tablecloth. But, to Master Leonardo's agitation, none knew how to use it or what to do with it. Some went to sit on it. Some to blow their noses in it. Some to throw playfully at each other. Yet others to wrap up viands and secrete them in their pouch or pocket. And after the meal was finished, and the main tablecloth dirtied as ever before, Master Leonardo confided to me his despair his invention would neer catch on.

'And too, this same week, Master Leonardo has suffered further setback at table. He had for one meal devised a salad dish, and had in mind that the great bowl containing it would be passed from person to person, each taking some small quantity from it. In its midst were quail eggs with the roes of sturgeon and little onions of Mantua, the which was laid out on and surrounded by succulent-looking leaves of lettuce from Bologna. But when the serving-person placed it before Lord Lodovico's Guest of Honour, Cardinal Albufiero of Ferrara, the Cardinal grasped at all its midst with the fingers of both hands and with the greatest rapidity consumed all the eggs, all the roes, all the onions; then took the leaves of lettuce to wipe his spattered face, and replaced them, thus tarnished, in the bowl – the which, the serving-person knowing no better, was then offered to My Lady D'Este. Master Leonardo was beside himself with anguish at such happening and I do feel it his salad bowl will not make much appearance more at table.'

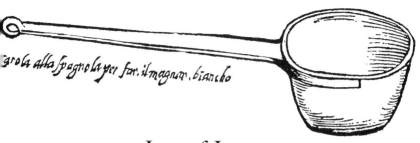

arola alla spagnola per far il magnan, biancho

Leg of Loon

Leg of loon is the best part of a loon – just as a boiled loon is preferable to a roasted loon, so is the leg of a loon more desirable than breast of loon. A loon should be hung for six weeks before being used, then it should be boiled in fresh garlic waters with no other flavouring than a little of pepper. And then it should be left to cool in a little rose-water, and as it starts to turn green then it should be consumed.*

*Testing this dish provided us with a small problem as our local pollaio *claimed not to have had a loon in stock for over 40 years. We eventually prevailed upon Conte Mario Alberti the noted gourmet and hunter to shoot a brace for us on the Tuscan property of Duca Simone di San Clemente, where is to be found one of the few surviving colonies of loons in Italy. (We are told the bird is more prevalent in the South of Spain.) We were prepared to hang our loons for six weeks as Leonardo directed but the poor birds were looking so unhappy after only two weeks that we decided to cook them then. The one loon we boiled in plain water with four cloves of garlic and a little pepper, the other loon we roasted. The boiled loon we removed from the pot after an hour and a half, then sprinkled with rose-water, and as anyway it had acquired a greenish hue while hanging we did not wait for this to develop into any brighter shade but carved it there and then. Both leg and breast we found quite inedible – tough and tasteless – and so far as the roast loon went we could only manage a little of its crispy skin. Its flesh was just as the boiled loon's. Perhaps it was our fault for not hanging the birds the full six weeks prescribed, or perhaps in the 500 years intervening between the writing of the recipe and our testing it the quality of loons has changed. Or perhaps, even, Leonardo meant domestic loons, not wild loons.*

73

padella

Bernardo's Boiled Cow Legs

I have watched Master Bernardo* boiling his cows' legs and always he performs this task in the same and curious manner – which is that he stands the legs of cows upright in his pot with cloths tied at each end to stop the marrows being released – which part, he claims, is best of any cow and does contain most value to our body's own well-being. With this I do agree, though I am not at one with Master Bernardo in the method that he does serve these boiled cow legs with marrows in them, just bones with all the flesh boiled off, for he does serve them whole and not chopped up and therefore for to drain the marrow from them makes all at table look like playing some ancient trumpets and if they do not have the strength to hold the leg aloft for long its downfall causes dreadful damage to themselves, the table and their goodly neighbours. But taste be good.

Bernardo Maggi di Abbiategrasso, master-carpenter at the Sforza Court, was also responsible for creating the sceneries designed by Leonardo for pageants and spectacles presented at the Castello. A man of vast size and strength, according to the poet Bellincioni (who would write parts for giants for him to perform in his plays) it might not have occurred to him that what was possible for him to eat was not always so suited to his guests of lesser size.

Merry Almond Soup

Boil some* young turnips in a pan containing a cooked sheep's head; mash them up afterwards with salt, pepper and cumin seed; mix in an egg to bind together and make into balls and shapes covered with bread-crumbs – in the middle of each ball and shape placing a tender cooked testicle of sheep. Place all in the oil-pot to become hard and brown on the outside, and serve. I know of no reason why this famous dish of Milan is called Merry Almond Soup.

Leonardo, like the other two writers on cookery in the Italy of his day, rarely defined his quantities more exactly than this. Always it was 'some' or 'a little' or 'half a handful'. This was probably because weights and measures varied so drastically from one Italian town to another. The smallest weight, the scruple, varied from the equivalent of 1.25 grams (one twenty-fourth of an ounce) in Rome, to 1.4 grams in Florence and 1.5 grams in Milan. Units of measure were just as confusing, the most common of them, the braccio (or arm) varying from the equivalent of 25 cms in the south of Italy to 45 in the north.

Sealion*

There are many who shun from eating this creature because of the gentle and pitiful look of its face. And those who are able to overcome this squeamishness – and who number among their ranks the smelly people of Ravenna and my friend Etero Alandi (who disguises it in prunes and a sweet and sour sauce) – receive little compensation for their dalliance at table with the animal. It is tough and foul-smelling and in my opinion only to be considered as food in a dire emergency. Its smell also is the reason why I will not approach within sight of Ravenna, for there, all day long, the people of this part are boiling the blubber of sealions to make their notorious laxative,** and also giving the blubber to their children to chew, which is why they grow up stinking of fish, and why they can never rid their bodies of this stench, and consequently find only each other to marry.

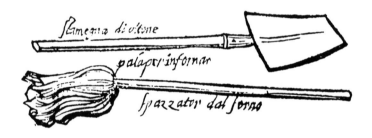

*In the fifteenth century seals, sealions and other allied species – often referred to by mariners as monsters – were a common phenomenon of the Adriatic coast of Italy. Today sealions in the Mediterranean are restricted to a small island off the east coast of Sardinia where a six-foot-long variety faces extinction not from the cook-pot but from the pollution of passing vessels which is causing them to change colour and abort their young.

**The famous 'Purga di Ravenna' which is sold in bright red boxes throughout all rural districts of Italy.

On the Correct Positioning of Diseased Guests at Table

Those guests with the most dire disease, and by this I mean not the Plague, but those with Scrophula or Pox, as well as those given to Wasting and Shrinking, and others covered in Sores and open wounds should not be sat (unless they be the sons of Popes or nephews of high Cardinals) beside My Lord, but instead are quite fit company for those of lesser rank and foreign notables with whom they may be sat between.

Those diseased of Hiccoughs and rife with Sniffles, those with Fits and Fidgets, and others with Delusions, My Lord also prefers to have apart from him (unless they be the sons of Popes or nephews of high Cardinals), for with them conversation can be tiresome. Nor should they be sat beside each other for that same reason, but rather, leavened with the lesser Members of the Court.

But guests with Bites, and dwarves and hump-backs, the halt and those who cannot move of their volition and of necessity are carried to the table, as well as those with swollen heads or heads too small My Lord does find acceptable and may be sat beside him.

Now to those with Plague. They must be sat apart, the table for them laid within My Good Lord's sight (but not his touch) and made of meanest wood that afterwards you burn, likewise the vessels that they ate from are destroyed, and those that served them are relieved of service for a thirty-day to see if Plague strikes them, then if all's well with them by then they can restart their duties; but if Plague-ridden they are dismissed forthwith for good of all.

On the Requirements of a Good Kitchen*

Firstly, [one needs] a constant source of fire. Then a constant supply of water that boils. Then a floor that is forever clean. Then Devices for Cleaning, Grinding, Slicing, Peeling and Cutting. Then a Device for keeping Stinks and Stenches away from the kitchen and ennobling it with a Sweet and Smokeless atmosphere. And then Musick, for men work better and more happily where there is Musick. And finally a Device for eliminating frogs from the barrels of drinking water.

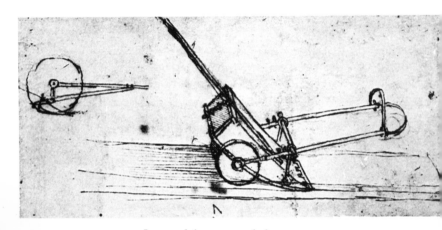

Leonardo's razor and sharpener.

The significance of this entry is that it also appears (though without the endpiece on Frogs) in the Copy MS of Leonardo's writings (made presumably when the original MSS were in Pompeio Leoni's hands) that has been in the Barberini Collection of the Vatican Library for nearly four hundred years. While this cannot substantiate the Codex Romanoff as a whole it can certainly be counted as one further proof of the Codex's genuineness.

White Pudding

This is not a dish for those who have the Pest, nor yet for those with troubled hearts. It is a very heavy dish indeed, bad for those with liver complaints and gall-stones too, and injurious to the eyesight and nerves of all. You peel the skins off almonds and pestle them in your mortar. Now pound the breasts of one half dozen capons, mix with a little milk of goat and press all through your sieve. Stir with your almond paste and add some twenty albumen of egg, some white bread-crumbs with a little fatty broth and pass all through your sieve into the frying pot. Sprinkle after but a while with rosewater and pips of Pomegranate and serve it up to eat,* and I have told Battista that if she does ever serve it up again in this household I shall not be there to serve again.

*As we know, not everything that Leonardo wrote into his Note Books was original or of his own thinking. He would copy down whole pages of other people's works (compare his abridgement of Aesop's Fables) or make notes of those works. This dish, in its translation from Latin to Italian, is almost word for word the same as the dish of the same name in Platina's De Honesta Voluptate et Valetudine (first published in 1475 when Leonardo was working in Florence) and a copy of which we know from Leonardo's own admission (Codex Atlanticus 210 r.a.) he had amongst his belongings when he moved from Milan to Florence in 1500 – though the copy Leonardo had is more likely to have been the 1487 edition published in Verona by which time it had become known that 'Platina' was in reality Bartolomeo Sacchi, librarian of the Vatican under Pope Sixtus IV, who had in fact copied down many of his recipes from a little-known MS by a cook called Maestro Martino da Como in the employ of service of the Patriarch of Aquilea. Nor should we overlook the possibility that Leonardo could have obtained the recipe directly from Sacchi before the latter died of the plague in 1481.

On Saffron in Wine

Saffron added to wine makes you very drunk and foul-smelling as well as making the wine taste most strange. As there is no receipt which instructs you to add saffron to wine I am surprised that my friend Gaudio Fullente so frequently offers it to one, but then as he is drunk and foul-smelling at all times it is possible I am wrong in my condemnation of his drink and it is he for whom I should have contempt.

Elder Flower Pie
(*Torta di Sambuco*)*

Mix elder flowers with the ingredients described in the recipe for White Pudding – but the mixture has to be thicker to consume all the flowers. This dish is not very nutritious but persons addicted to it and who eat it often find it gives them much happiness.

Compare the wording of Leonardo's recipe with that for Torta Sambucea in Platina's Honesta Voluptate: *'Loribus Sambuci omnia illa misceto: quae in torta alba Comemorium 9. Spiffior in haec copositio q'illa debetesse: quo flores in partes omnes transserantur & spiarum alit: & tarde digeritur: laetiores, t'ame crebro uesce tes facit.' – The similarities are so remarkable that one must assume Leonardo had access to Platina's book upon this occasion also. As Leonardo did not teach himself to read in the Latin tongue until 1495–6 this is helpful to us in dating the writing of his recipe.*

Porridge with Sprouts

I am told this is the speciality of, and considered a great delicacy among the people who dwell on the marshes around Padua which – they having the reputation they do, and looking like they do – makes me most suspicious of the dish.

The sprout-tops are cut from the sprout-bush and then brushed to remove the web of the sprout-spiders who breed in their midst – which web, so they say, if even consumed in the smallest quantity can produce in the consumer a continuous nausea which can turn into his total paralysis – however Fonzo Ghiberti assures us there is an antidote for this condition if the afflicted sprout-eater can be made to bend over an inhalation of chopped hyssop leaves.

Amongst the marsh-dwellers of Padua the cleaned and brushed sprouts are placed in boiling water for but three minutes, then drained and left to cool, and then dipped with fingers into a mixture of cold porridge.

Amongst those who inhabit the valley of the Po a different method is used. The sprouts are boiled for three hours, or sometimes even overnight, and then the smelly sprout-water – for that is all there is by then – is mixed into the porridge and drunk as company to crushed frogs legs.

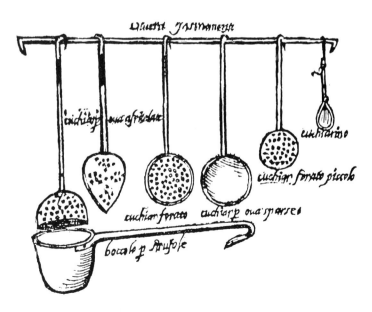

My Favourite Porridge Dishes*

❀ Slices of Porridge with Herrings and Rings of Raw Onion. (You behead and boil the herrings in a casserole first.)

❀ Slices of Cold Porridge with Hard-boiled Eggs and Pilchards. (Take care to roast the porridge-fingers just before serving, and to pour a little oil on their surface before you lay down the pilchards and eggs.)

❀ Porridge with Prunes. (Sometimes I add a little cinnamon.)

❀ Black Porridge with Roasted Anchovy Butter from Trento. (You must use equal parts of white wine and water when mixing this porridge, and spread the butter on it liberally.)

❀ Porridge with Pigs-feet and the Cheese of Mantua. (You roll out your porridge very fine on a marble slab and cut it into little pie-cases which you stuff with the cooked and sliced feet and the cheese, and seal with your fingers. Then you place the little pie-balls in your pan of pig-fat until they are golden-brown and crisp.)

*It does seem very odd that someone as outspoken as Leonardo normally was on the subject of porridge should be recommending these variations of the dish. In the circumstances one might perhaps consider that by the words 'My favourite' he was actually referring to someone else altogether whose name he had forgotten to add – possibly his friend Luca Pacioli who was a great protagonist of the substance.

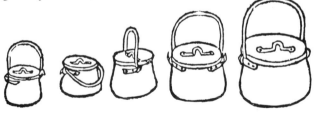

diuersi caldari

Pig Tails in Porridge*

This is of my own devising even though my ancient friend Massimo Cippolini claims I stole it from his kitchen.

Take the tails of thirty pigs, clean and debone them in such a way that the outside skin does not become unduly broken and there remain hollow chambers throughout the tail. Now fill these chambers – with what it matters little, an anchovy, some lean pork meat – whatever is to hand. Now place these tails inside a pot and cover them with soft cold water to which you've added some onions with carnation seeds – but pound those seeds. Boil slowly for an hour, then remove pig tails and dry them well and pass them through your mangle. Leave them to revivify for some two hours, then wrap a thinly rolled porridge round each one and place on oven rack for one half hour – or just until the porridge does turn brown and crispy. These are a great favourite with the children of my father's family and I do always make them when I visit them.

*Leonardo's word is in fact 'polenta' but for the English edition of this work we have asked that it should be translated as 'porridge' with which English readers are more familiar. Both polenta and porridge have been the basic foods of humanity from the beginning of time – far more so than bread – polenta being made of ground maize left to dry in the sun then mixed with water, porridge being oatmeal with water, or sometimes, as with the French bouillie, with equal proportions of ground maize and oatmeal. But the end result is the same, a basic commodity to which any number of different flavourings can be added. More porridge was eaten than any other dish in the Europe of Leonardo's time.

barachino   frifritor   padella vuota

Pickled Birds

The best way that I know to pickle little birds is that you pluck and boil them in a wine with vinegar and herbs and salt and leave them thus and boil them up again once every month until all bones are soft – which normally is three months in the case of larks, and six in case of loon.

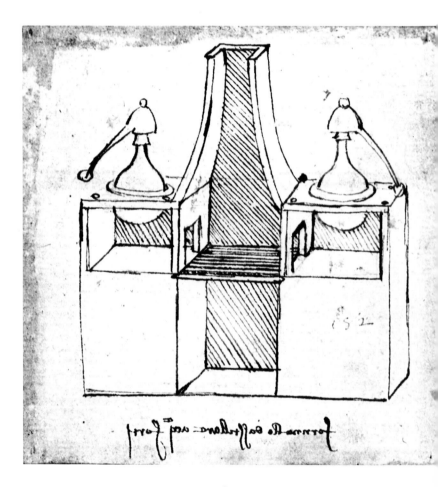

Pierced Pigs' Ears

You should remove both ears from your pig, and then you should singe them and scrub and scrape them (their insides especially) most thoroughly before you place them in boiling waters to which a carrot has been added (one carrot to each ear some do prefer). Then you should place them on skewers interleaved with bay-leaves and prunes and hold over the fire for two minutes before serving with a dish of porridge.

The taste of the ears of a pig from Padua is said to be much superior to that of a pig from elsewhere, but as I cannot imagine myself travelling to Padua just to prove or disprove this assertion I must needs await until such time as I have other more serious business in those parts. And meantime, I am well content with the pigs of Milan, and their ears.

On Feasts

My Lord does spurn the simple foods I offer for his Feastings and does insist on his barbarian dishes. My duty is to do my best to dress them: sweet-smelling plants and dragon-flies and fountains everywhere; the sound of crickets from without; rose-waters for his diners' hands and gold-dust for his turnips; statues of brightest marzipan and pies with feet; coloured jellies in the shape of Palaces; trumpet players, timbal players and ostriches that roam around – he shall have ALL. And yet I would exchange this all for but to see one een simple dish like I suggest upon his table.

LEFT: The revolutionary sideboard which Leonardo made for Beatrice D'Este had containers for iced wine and iced orange juice as well as a hot plate in the centre. Cod. Atl. fol. 335r–b.

The Machines I have yet to Design for my Kitchens

- one for plucking ducks
- one for cutting a pig into cubes
- one for mashing
- one for grinding a pig
- one for pressing a sheep

Yet how shall I work them ?* By wind or by water ? By cogs and by cranks ? By oxen or by peasant-power ?

*The motive power to operate his machines was Leonardo's biggest frustration, and why it was so frequently out of all proportion to the end result (i.e. the giant nut-cracker operated by three horses [see page 46]). It has always baffled us how, seeing steam go to waste so much in his kitchens, he never invented the steam engine. All the ingredients were available to him, including the piston, but somehow he just never got them together.

A Christmas Pudding

(This is the receipt of my friend Atalante Miglioitti the musician.) Skin, debone and pulp seven large white fish, mix with the crumbs from seven light-coloured loaves and whole grated white truffle, bind this all together with the albumen of seven hens eggs and steam in a strong cloth bag for a day and a night. When you eat it take care not to choke on any Holy Relics that may have been secreted in it.

Roasted Peacock

The cooking of peabirds involves much time and many deceits. To kill a peacock you do adopt the same procedure as with a goat – you cut its throat and then with a point you penetrate its brain to let the blood run out. And then you hang it in a fig tree for one night to make it tender, its empty body stuffed with nettles, and with weights attached to both its legs.* Now you cut the skin on the surface from the throat to the tail and peel it off together with the feathers and the legs still attached. Keep this carefully to one side. You place the carcase of the bird in the oven, its insides stuffed with carnation seeds, sweet-smelling herbs sprinkled over it, and – what is most important of all – its neck and head wrapped in white cloth which must be kept wet all the time of cooking so that they are not distorted by the heat.

When the bird is cooked – it will take two to three times as long as a capon for its meat is that much more tough – take it off the spit and dress it with its own skin which you had placed aside; and to make the bird look as though it is standing fix legs of iron upon your table-top and place the bird upon them – the iron should be pushed right through the bird from head to tail but not be seen. And now you may add wool and camphor into the bird's beak and light it. (Gallio does not do this because he is so afraid of fire.)

Now you may make a pretence at carving the bird for your guests, but in fact what you will serve them will be the meat of peahens which you will have cooked at the same time as the cock, but the meat of which is more tender and so more acceptable to your guests.

For those who suffer from liver and spleen the eating of peabirds is not to be advised. The meat is heavy and not very nutrious.

Salai's Egg Dish

There are still those who, like the ignorants of antiquity, will place an egg in boiling waters and then, after so many hours when they believe it to be cooked, will break it open and cast out its yellow centre like the stone from a plum. Salai's Egg Dish therefore is not for them as it requires that both parts of the cooked egg be used. You mash them together, adding salt, pepper and finely-chopped parsley-flower, with a little olive oil to bind it together. Then I do not know what you do, as Salai will not tell me. But I have seen him cowering in dark corners some nights eating a mixture which looks very like this on his porridge.

*This passage occurs almost word for word in the original edition of Valturio's De Re Mangiare published by Joannes Nicolai de Verona in 1472 (and of which there is an incomplete copy in the Vatican Library). It is omitted in Ramusio's translation for the Milan edition of 1483 so Leonardo must have copied it from the original edition some time after 1497 when he had taught himself Latin – unless, of course, a friend translated it for him before that date.

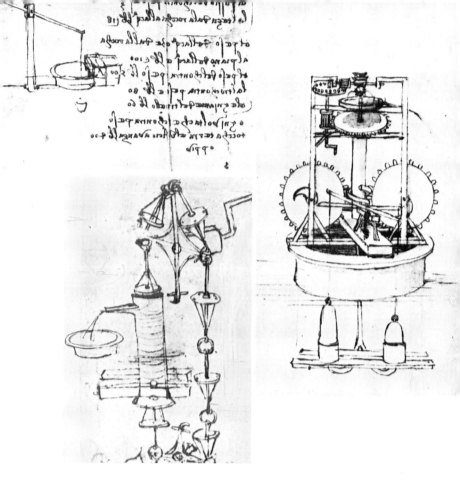

Leonardo's device for working out the cubic capacity of eggs
(and at the same time accurately counting up to one half
dozen of them) was not used extensively in Kitchens until
Escoffier's time several centuries later. Likewise, his device
for liquidising ancient eggs and turning the putrifactive matter resultant into a poisonous gas was not used (actually by
the Germans) until the days of the Western Front in World
War 1. But his Massive Device originally intended for grinding egg shell into powder for coating meat balls has played an
important part in the Murano glass industry since the early
sixteenth century.

Cod. Atl. fol. 386v–b. Cod. Atl. fol. 386r–b.

Sheeps' Testicles
with Honey and Cream

Take the testicles of a sheep and remove from them their outer skins and leave the testicles to soak in cold waters for some hours. Now cut or grate them into thin slices, season with salt and pepper (and, Pietro Monti submits, also a little saffron to give them a less unhealthy colour) and cook them in a butter until such time as you can feel a tenderness in them. Now leave to cool, and when cooled pour a little cream and hot honey over them and serve. This is the *correct* way to serve sheeps' testicles, although my Lord Lodovico insists on them being hot when served to him, and considers them thus the ideal accompaniment to the mashed turnips on which he so dotes.

Pietro Monto submits also that, like a white truffle from Alba, a sheep's testicle may be grated over other foodstuffs to their advantage, producing, curiously, a flavour not unlike that of white truffles.

Cocks' Combs in Crumbs

Take care that your cock is a large one, over twelve months old and with its head standing 6ocms or more from the ground, before you remove his comb. And remember always to peel the outer skin and then squeeze repeatedly to drain off all blood before placing it in the boiling water with twelve coriander seeds and the juice of half a lemon.

The mulehead Salai recommends that ten cocks are needed for each person to be fed, and also he says that because the cocks become white with cooking and not attractive to the eye they should be placed on the serving dish interleaved with slices of a vegetable that has some colour –

raw carrots carved in the shape or cocks-combs, or beetroot –
before the crumbs are sprinkled over them. The composition
of his dish appeals little to me.

Battered Loon

A Loon, that most tasty of all small birds, is cooked in its
own juice, then lightly battered and placed in a pan of boiling
pig-fat for but half a minute. It emerges crisp and ready to be
coated with pepper and honey before eating.

Goat's Head Pie
(*For Poor Persons and Rough People*)

Cleave the goat's head into two, lengthwise. Remove the
brains and tongue. Boil what remains in water to which one
carrot and a sprig of chervil has been added. After three
hours place – with all the liquid – in a dish lined and then
covered with a hard porridge crust. Serve with a green sauce
made of the brains and tongue cut up finely and cooked with
twice as much their weight of parsley flower.

On Sadness from Porridge

I am sad because I have been looking at dishes of porridge all
the day. It looks so *dull*.

Four Simple Soups

1 SOUP OF CAPERS

Boil some handfuls of soft fresh fruits in a pig-stock and after a while strain through your horse-sieve. Now use your capers to spell out the words *Zuppa di Cappero* [Caper Soup] on its top. This way the capers taste much fresher than if they had been boiled in your pig-stock, and also the dish is immediately identifiable to your guests.

2 SOUP OF BERRIES

You make this like you make Soup of Capers but at the end instead of using capers you decorate it with berries which spell out the words *Zuppa di Bacci* (Berry Soup). Do not forget to do this as otherwise your gests may think you are serving them with caper soup again.

3 SOUP OF ORANGES AND LEMONS

This is very different to Soup of Capers or Soup of Berries. You make a stock of two hens and strain it well through your horse-sieve, now mix into it the juice from a basket of oranges and lemons which you have beaten some eggs into. And this soup you may serve hot or cold. Battista when she makes Soup of Oranges and Lemons prefers to leave out the oranges, but I prefer it with them.

4 I do forget this.

Storks and Cranes

There are very few who eat storks or cranes these days. I am wondering the reason of this.

Dish of Rawnesses

This is for those who have eaten of too many rich foods for too many days and whose digestions have need of a rest. They will have need of

- An apricot
- A carrot
- An onion from Venice
- A radish from Cremona
- Some green beans from Tesco
- Some olives that are green
- Some olives that are black
- A hard-boiled hen-egg
- And a small white mouse*

– wash, peel or scrape these as befits each to make them clean and wholesome, but do not cook them in any way whatsoever. Cut them into shapes and slices and arrange them on a dish in an interesting pattern so that never do the same two colours touch to each other.

The dish is sufficient to satisfy all requirements of the body.

*We are of course left wondering about this small white mouse. Was it to be washed, peeled or scraped? Was Leonardo really advocating a return to the decadent eating habits of Imperial Rome? In our copy of the MS he uses the word 'topo' which undoubtedly means 'mouse' – had he meant 'mousse' he would have used the Italian word 'alce'. The nearest guess we can make is that his 'topo' is a mis-spelling for 'toppo' meaning a log, or tree-stump, and that is what he actually meant – bearing in mind his experiments with the unfortunate Salai, when he caused Salai to live on a diet of grasses and trees to prove their usefulness to man, and coming to the conclusion that the palm tree was the only possibly edible one, or rather, the heart of palm as eaten since Roman times – and which would have been perfectly acceptable in his 'dish of Rawnesses'.

Dead Rabbit

Skin a dead rabbit and gut it then place it on a high spit to cook slowly, and when you think it is completely dead sprinkle a little salt and pepper over it and serve with a medium stiff porridge.

NOTE: all parts of a dead rabbit may be eaten.

On the Reason so Few Persons eat Storks or Cranes

It is because they are afraid of the snakes that the storks and cranes consume.

The Dishes I do Abhor
(but which still good Battista does insist to serve me)

JELLIED GOAT

Battista tells me, firstly you must make a 'gelatine'. You take the feet of forty cows, skinned, filletted and cleaned. You then do leave them just to soak in cold waters for four hours, then place them in a pan of strong vinegar, white wines, water and a small anchovy. Cook this on a gentle fire, stirring it and skimming the top carefully, and after a further four hours add some pepper and some cinnamon – enough to thin out the odour of the cooking feet. Continue thus until the liquid has been reduced to one third itself, then add ten albumen of egg that you have whipped and strain it thrice through linen cloths and pour resultant liquid over goat – which you must place upon a dish that can be left in some chamber of cold humidity until the gelatine does set and you can see your goat quite clearly through it. My friend Voconio does always have one such dish as this within his larder so it may be proferred to his company at any time without a further cooking. There is no such dish kept in my larder and Voconio himself does not eat his because he finds it accentuates his bile.

HEMP BREAD

This is a dangerous dish indeed which for many years I have eschewed – yet have as many friends who long for it any cost alway. You cook the seeds of hemp until the peel comes off quite voluntarily. You pound these peel-less seeds with just their equal of fresh cleaned almonds. You place the mixture through your sieve, then mix it with a little honey, salt and pepper, and so boil it. Now, place one layer of bread slices at the bottom of some pot. Spread of the cooked hemp some over them. Place yet another layer of bread slices on top of this and spred yet more hemp on them. Continue doing such until you do achieve ten layers of the each – then, sprinkle sweet herbs over all and place a great weight on top of this for some nights to compress it for your satisfaction.

ELDER TREE PUDDING

Leave to soak in water for but one hour some flowers of the elder tree. Drain them, then pound them with peeled almonds and mix all with the same amount of bread crumbs soaked and coloured with the brightest saffron. Some now will add two beaten eggs, sour grapes and grated cheese, but I say it is unnecessary : boil it as it is. Labio my friend does every time refuse this dish, not only for reason of its unseemly taste, but also for its smell. But there are those who declare it very good persons who suffer from melancholy and haemhorroids.

WHITE MOSQUITO PUDDING

Chop well skinned almonds with a pinch of elder flowers and pass them through the sieve. Cook slowly on the fire for half and hour, add honey, breast of capon boiled and pound this all. Sprinkle with your rose-water and serve immediately. This dish takes a long time to digest and is not good for persons who suffer from colic or gripe. But it is helpful to those who have the Pest and those who ask me why it's so-called I cannot help.

A SPANISH DISH

Place on your fire a pan with some rice flour (of the first quality) mixed with milk of goat (not too close to flame so it does not absorb the smoke). Not cut to slithers a breast of capon you just have killed and half cook him, then place him in your mortar and pound him twice (or at the most three times). Mix with him now his weight in honey and place him in the boiling pan of goated flour. He will be ready in but a quarter hour. – My friend Galba has oft offered me this dish covered with sugars from his estate in Sicily, and while this has caused in me a feeling of great nausea Tridento asserts he has never eaten any dish more delicate. – Stay off this dish if truly that you can. It is of little nourishment, it causes dizziness and nausea, and weakens both the eyesight and the knees. There is a tavern in the midst of Florence where no other dish is served – and every single person in this tavern is a madman.

fuochone

INEDIBLE TURNIPS

Battista cooks her turnips beneath the ashes then she waits
for them to cool and slices them most finely, and slices even
finer still some cheese that is not too mature. And then she'll
grease a pan with lard and place within it first a layer of said
fine-sliced cheese, and then a layer of the cooked and sliced
turnips, and then another layer of cheese and so on till the
pan is full. Sprinkle lard and herbs upon its top and cook for
half an hour. – Now, be warned. This dish it is not good for
you. It makes my friend Irzio wake up in the night shouting
because of acute pains in his thighs. You are best to give it to
greedy Dominziano who will eat anything, or to the wrest-
lers in the taverns who claim they thrive upon it.

EEL BALLS

You peel an eel and then you empty all its insides out and cut
it into half-thumb size piece and cook these pieces – a bay-
leaf in between each piece – upon the spit, and now you keep
them moist continuously by pouring brine all over them.
And then when these are cooked you wrap each piece in
some small soft porridge flavoured with a little cinnamon and
place them in your oven until their crusts get brown. – This
dish if eaten often can cause madness.

TENDRIL PIE

You must pick tendrils* that are from trees or fence-posts not visited by squirrels – for the droppings of squirrels, who love all tendrils dearly, do create a bitter taste. Boil the tendrils in tied bunches and after ten minutes so remove them from the water and cut them into tiny pieces (you can also do this with red roses, or you can mix tendrils and red roses – provided they are roses that have not been visited by squirrels). Now you add fresh cheese cut into small pieces, and some breast of pig (first boiled then pounded). You place this mixture in a pan, well-greased with other pig, and lined with a fine porridge. You place the pan upon the fire, with countless holes you make upon its top, and when the smell of tendrils, or the smell of tendrils mixed with roses, fills the air you sprinkle all with some rose-water and you serve. – This dish, if ate too oft, will also cause a madness. Sometimes you hear of entire families having died from eating it.

BOILED INTESTINES

It does not matter what intestines, you clean and wash them well, then boil them with a bone of pig, and when they do look cooked you cut them into pieces not too big and unite them with some pounded sage and ginger and just a little saffron. You mix this with some fatty broth and sour grapes, you strain it through your horse-sieve, and boil it on a charcoal flame – stirring all the time with wooden spoon, for up to sixty minutes. Now this, when served upon a plate, is the most heavy liquid and though there are those who do say it's nutrious and a little aphrodisiac, and good for those who suffer with a liver or a hear, I do myself prefer to use it as a glue.

*Leonardo probably means vine-shoots. Anything, to him, which clung to something else, he referred to as 'tendril'.

For Salai to Note

The morrow will come to dine in Corte Vecchio:

My colleague Donato Bramante*
Georgio Merula
Giovanni Battagio da Lodi
Galeazzo Sanseverino
Matteo Bandelli
Luca Pacioli
and Sabba da Castiglione di Pietro Alemanni

Battista will make for them a Mixed Cow Pie and we will drink the wine of Vigevano.

Bramante the architect of Santa Maria delle Grazie, Merula the Greek scholar and translator of Plato, Battagio da Lodi an architect and gentleman of Verona, Sanseverino the drunken womanizing General of Ludovico, Bandelli the novelist – also on Ludovico's payroll, Pacioli Leonardo's mathematics mentor, and Pietro Alemanni the Florentine Ambassador. Except for the last-named they were amongst Leonardo's closest friends in Milan. The presence of Luca Pacioli in the company suggests that the meal took place in or after 1496 when Pacioli first came to Milan from Pavia.

Marzipan

The marzipan made for me, for my carvings, by the Sisters of Santa Corona, is of pounded almonds, honey and the whites of eggs in quantities that only they know, and baked in their ovens for such length of time as only the Mother Superior decides. I have noted, sadly, that My Lord Lodovico and his Court digest the carvings I give to them to the last crumb and now I am set to find some other substance their palates shall less appreciate that my Works may survive. Here again I think of my Blanc-mange, if I can but give it some more stability, and mayhap with some bitter-tasting matters in it the palate will reject. But again, Fazio Cardano, subjecting my recipe to his careful analysis, has vouchsafed the outer surface of my blanc-mange could, after a period of time, be capable of producing some heavy green mould to obscure the fineness of my designs. – And this the marzipan has never done, nor has it ever had the time to.

Shoulder of Serpent

I know of but one man who still serves serpent at his table and that is Ambrogio Varese da Rosate the alleged astrologist,* so I am safe to say that I know of none better than his which he does accompany with an onion and a carrot. Neither will Ambrogio divulge to me from whence come his serpents, nor will he deny that he who supplies them to him will tell him of their source or who does breed them, nor yet have I seen one whole upon his table to describe its shape. And yet, to tell about its taste: it has not one, but many.

*in fact Court Astrologist to Ludovico and a constant sparring partner of Leonardo who ridiculed his beliefs and predictions and Ludovico's reliance upon them.

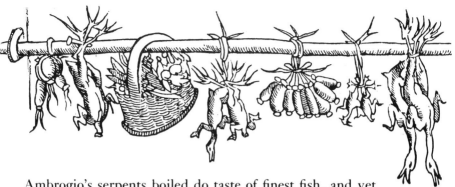

Ambrogio's serpents boiled do taste of finest fish, and yet pot-roasted that same beast – and served with roasted leeks – will seem more like the flesh of boar. And in his serpent soup lie tastes of fish and boar combined, and more. And further still, the testicles that he serves separate, finely sliced and with a light mint sauce, are twice the size of goats and shelter twice the taste. But what that taste may be, of serpent's testicles, I dare not try to say : it is sweet, it is sour, it is strong, it is subtle, nor yet can any cook improve it anyhow. Then most of all I do prefer of serpent shoulder. Here which follows, is Ambrogio's recipe for a serpent shoulder :

Take a shoulder of serpent and debone it and stuff the hole that then is made with olives and fresh fruits. Sew this up and leave it in a juice of prunes that covers all of it for two nights long. Then place it on your spit and turn till all the outer side is black denoting it is ready to be served – which must be with onions and some carrots boiled separate though in a serpent stock.

– That is Ambrogio's recipe, I think.

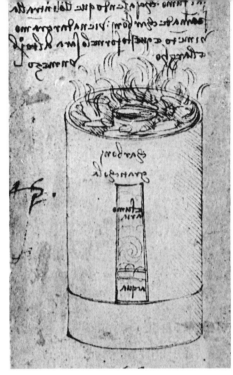

The wood-burning barbecue Leonardo designed for
Ludovico Sforza in 1491 is still the basis of the model pro-
duced by the Leonardo Patent Barbecue and Divan Co. of
Vinci to-day.
Cod. Atl. fol. 306r–c–d.

Dish of Newts

Dredge from your frog-pond some sievefuls of newts which
are not yet formed into frogs – it is in the fifth week of their
development that they should be gathered for it is then that
they taste the best. To render them dead place them for but a
moment in a pan of fiercely steaming waters, then cleanse
them thoroughly under cold running waters and lay the
bodies out to dry on a cloth which will absorb any of these
waters left upon them. Now sprinkle them with a fine flour
flavoured with salt and pepper (or salt and coriander), shake
them in a dry sieve to be rid of any unnecessary flour, and

pour them into a pan of boiling oil of olive to become a little brown. Again lay them out on a cloth which can absorb the unnecessary oil and when that is achieved then they are ready to be consumed. A little of lemon juice poured on them is the habit of some advocates of this dish. But there are also others who, when told the content of the dish they have just eaten, do go pale and leave the table in a haste.

Boiled Coot

It is of import to skin a coot, for a coot's skin is ugly, oily, foul-smelling, and unpalatable to all except wild dogs. Coot fat, on the other hand, which may be produced from over-boiling a coot, is held in great esteem on its own, or spread on garlic porridge.

Dish of Mixed Knuckles

You will need one sheep, one pig, one cow, three lemons, a little pepper and some olive oil. Remove the knuckles from the legs of all beasts, soak them overnight in the lemons, pepper and olive oil, then roast them gently until a dark golden brown, and serve them on a bed of hardening porridge. This simple dish makes one of My Lord Lodovico's most favourite meals.*

*This dish we know, from Matteo Bandelli's account of the event, was served at the great feast Ludovico gave in 1493 upon the visit to Milan of the German Emperor Maximilian who had just married, in Innsbruck, Ludovico's niece Bianca Maria Sforza – and was served not just at the feast in the Castello, but also, to mark the occasion, was distributed free to the whole populace of Milan from carts that Leonardo and the architect Bramante had jointly designed in the likeness of giant eagles on wheels.

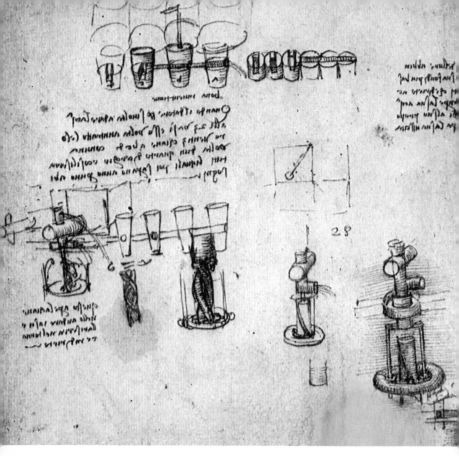

The operation of Leonardo's original left-handed corkscrew clearly made it the forerunner of the tap in to-day's Box of Wine – drink could be poured out of the bottle while the device was in it.

Cod. Atl. fol. 362v–a.

Jelly Fish

Cook a gutted pike gently, making sure it is covered by water all the time. After four hours remove its skin and transfer it to another pan to cook in fresh waters for a further four hours. Let it cool, then place it in your jelly pot and pour over it a jelly made with water, wine vinegar and cows feet.

bestigliu

On Goats in Kitchens

I have no room for any goat in my kitchen. Alive it is
foul-smelling and devours everything, including my tables
and benches. Dead it is even more foul-smelling. To be rid of
goat-stink, be rid of the goat.

Anecdote

When Gregorio Pacioli, the sculptor of Madonnas from
Venice, was advised that the solution to the constipation
which had plagued him all his life lay in the regular consumption of grapes, he did not stop to question in what form
the grapes should be took, but chose the liquid form.
Thenceforth he drank every day six bottles of fine grape
wine, undiluted with honey or water. Nor until the end of
his life – which was twelve years in coming – did he suffer
further constipation. Nor yet – which was to the confoundment of the Senate of Venice and others – did he create
further Madonnas. It was to the Senate's confoundment as
he was, at the beginning of this period of time, beholden to
them for 36 Madonnas for which they had paid him much in
advance and now had to sit back and watch him spend their
ducats on his drinking. And shortly before he died Pacioli
confided to his brother that had he but known of grapes
earlier it would have removed all strain from his previous
life.

On Grasses

ITEM: if a cow eats grasses and nothing else, and if a sheep eats grasses and nothing else, and if they both do survive, and then if I eat cow and the sheep to no ill effect, why then should we all not eat grasses? Salai will help me to pursue the matter.*

*Yet again we are indebted to a letter (dated September 1493 in Annali di Firenze Vol XV p. 342) from the omnipresent Florentine Pietro Alemanni to the Signoria of Florence for a description of the events subsequent to this thought of Leonardo's:

'. . . For this last week Master Leonardo has caused his disciple Salai to resort to a diet exclusively of Grasses, in order, says the Maestro, to solve the Problem of Salvation in our world. Master Leonardo himself had been choosing the Grasses, washing them and cutting off parts of their roots, yet even after one day Salai was complaining he had been unable to digest any part of what was set before him. And Master Leonardo being in a great fury that the wretched Salai was refusing to digest his chosen Grasses, and hearing none of it that the poor man, nor any member of the human race, might be unable to digest them – withdrew to the kitchens to make more palatable. The contents of one bowl of Grasses he boiled, to another he added some oil and vinegar, a third he formed into small balls and placed on his roasting apparatus, and at the end of his labours he commanded his quivering pupil to eat of which and say which was his preference. The near-tearful youth first essayed the Grasses which were boiled and pronounced them as indigestible as the raw Grasses; then he placed in his mouth some of that which was covered in the oil and vinegar and spat it out forthwith. And now in a fury far greater than before Master Leonardo took a handful of the roasted grass balls and essayed to thrust them down the throat of Salai, whereupon Salai threw vomit all over the Maestro and the Maestro retired disgusted claiming that his greatest offering to mankind was wasted and ruined through the selfishness of his useless pupil. But then I do believe, Master Leonardo forgot totally of the experiment for some short time later I perceived him at his sketchbook detailing geometric outlines.'

Pot Tops

Upon every occasion that the pot goes over the fire it is necessary to cover it with wet linen which needs frequent changing to prevent the fire's smoke mingling with the contents of the pot and so changing its taste. This has been so for hundreds of years. Now I ask myself, could not a permanent cover be devised for the pot which would be as indestructible as the pot itself, always available, and not needing change? I shall make a design.

Horse Soup
(*Zuppa di Cavallo*)

This is the safest way of digesting a horse. It should be cooked in the same manner as Cow Soup, only with three onions in place of the three carrots. (One horse is normally sufficient to feed 200 persons.)

Frog Soup

Peel three frogs (for the skin of a frog is of no help to the digestion), then gut them (for the guts of a frog do secrete a multitude of poisons), now roll the corpses in honey and immerse them with a carrot and a cumin flower in a boiling stew bowl for an hour. Drain this through your sieve and you will have left a carrot of quite exceptional taste. (Gregorio Summus prefers his carrot when it has been cooked in proximity with sixteen or so snails of the Romagna, while Galeazzo Sanseverino will not eat any frog which has been touched or bitten by snails. He also advocates that the skins should be removed from the legs of the frog the day before they are cooked and they should be left thus to swim in milk and water all the night.)

pignatta granue *cucumaio*

Soup of Turnip-top

There are those who say that turnip-top and cabbage, in all forms solid whatsoever, are fit food for those of robust disposition only – slaughterers, stone-carriers, tillers in the field; and that librarians, invalids, small female persons and all those with delicate digestions do best not to avail themselves of such food.*

On the contrary I say the use of turnip-top and cabbage will turn a weak digestion strong through the value in its leaves which I have seen to make a sick goat sprightly once more, and a dying cow to come alive and dance.

But for those who have belief in that first theory then they may try the soup. Make the turnip-tops or cabbage leaves into bundles with horse-hairs tied around them. Plunge them into salted boiling waters and leave them thus for half an hour. The liquid drained can make a simple dish for Lent.

The wording of this passage does make one wonder whether the celebrated English cook Madame Beaton could have had access to Leonardo's MS. For she writes, in her Book of Household Management *(first published 1861): 'Cabbage is heavy and a long time digesting. It is only fit for robust and active persons; the sedentary or delicate should carefully avoid it.' – But for the most part the dishes and ingredients of Leonardo's recipes figure little in Madame Beaton's work.*

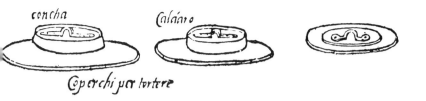

concha Calàaro

Coperchi per tortere

Further on Pot Tops

It is told me by good Bernardo, to whom I did speak of my
design for pot tops, that all My Lord's pots do in truth
already have such tops, and always have, but for many years
they have been misused by the scullions of the kitchens and
now they lie – to detriment of all that cooks – misshapen
without the castle walls where every night these scullions
meet to beat them loud and dance to this that they call music.
– Enough of this, each scullion will return his lid or work no
longer in these kitchens.

On the Benefits of
a Moderate Diet

I have writ before* (I think) that if you would keep your
health you should not eat unless you feel inclined, and
always should sup lightly; chew well, and let all you take be
simple and well-cooked. Now look at Fazio Cardano, he is
the strongest man at Court and yet does eat all day the richest
fares. Look at My Lord, his appetite for quantity goes undi-
minished – and he swallows all without one single chew. It
happens thus – to every rule there must exceptions be. Or
else maybe I'm wrong.

*In his collection of writings in Codex Atlanticus 78v.b. where he goes on
to say 'Be temperate with wine, take a little frequently, but not at other
than the proper meal-times, nor on an empty stomach; neither protract nor
delay your visit to the privy.'

On Simple Dishes

This which is spread upon my Lord Lodovico's table ashames my eyes. Every dish is a monstrous mess. Everything is *quantity*. This is the way barbarians ate. And yet how can I convince him this is so when he spurns my dish of noble sprouts nor yet can find the room upon his cloth for my prune with handsome carrot ? – For there is more beauty in a single sprout, more dignity in one small carrot than in twelve of his gold bowls piled high with meat and bones; there is more subtlety in one old prune, more nourishment in two green beans. What must I do to show My Lord so ? The quality of *simplicity* is what My Lord has need to rediscover. And not just he, but all throughout the land. For what do the people of Lombardy do when they make a pie of rabbit ? They disguise the tasteful rabbit with four other meats, with a dozen herbs, with the juices of twenty fruits. Equally, their pie of rabbit could be a pie of lark, a pie of thrush, a pie of pig. And the people of Todi, when they serve what they call their dish of frog, how much of a frog lies in it ? – But a mere tenth is frog, and all the rest is soup of pig, is herbs, is oils, is creams, is poor dead fruits and mushrooms – which taste not of themselves but of the pig and frog, just as the pig and frog tastes of them – and all of it, the whole, wrapped in a heavy crust of porridge as though the people of Todi feel their guilt at such a dish and wish to hide their shames from those to whom they offer it. I say if you serve a frog, let him look like a frog and taste like a frog. If you serve a rabbit let him look like a rabbit and taste like a rabbit. And as concerning My Lord Lodovico, if he wishes his dish of meat and bones then let it be displayed as such, not in one unrecognizable mass smothered in an indestructible sauce, but the meat in neat pieces in neat lines, the bones prettily arranged around them. For in My Lord's kitchens are men who will conceal the shape and taste of every pure thing that grows upon the earth, and until My Lord's kitchens can be liberated from these descendants of barbarians, or until such time as I can prove to them the wrongness of their ways and instruct them in the nobility of the single sprout, the single carrot, even the single unadorned bone, then so will My Lord's table remain the mess it is.

Boiled Eggs

Break your eggs into a pan of boiling waters, and as soon as the albumen turns white remove them from the pan on to your serving dish. Now cover them with a little honey, some sweet herbs, some rosewater, some sweet and sour wine and the juice of a pomegranate, and eat them with bread. Sometimes when Battista is in a haste she will serve me these eggs without any other decoration than a little salt and pepper and I have to admit I enjoy the dish just as much.

Broken Eggs

Break your eggs in a bowl and beat them up with a little water or milk, a little grated cheese, a little oil and butter, a little salt and pepper. Cook them very gently in a pan, stirring all the while, for not more than a minute. If you wish to have them green, add a little beetroot.*

*Despite the references to it in Calvi's Notizie dei professore di belli arti che fiorirono in Milano durante il governo dei Visconti e degli Sforza Part III (Borroni, Milan 1869) there is no other indication in Leonardo's own writings of his possible colour-blindness. He probably meant tops of beet.

Hard-boiled Eels

The secret of good hard-boiled eels, according to my friend Francesco Bramante, is that only their outer skins are removed before cooking and not their bones, and then they should not be in boiling waters for more than three minutes. True, it is impossible to digest the flesh because of this short period of cooking, but here again is Bramante's secret: now you may cut the eel into sections each the size of half a thumb, smother each in honey and suck one in your mouth for upwards of twenty minutes – and all that period of time be savouring the glorious taste of eel. This also accounts for Bramante moving his mouth all the time he is working; throughout the day he is sucking on his eels.

On Ridding your Kitchens of Pestilential Flies

The way to keep flies out of a kitchen is to sprinkle pepper over the room and especially over all carcasses hanging in it.

Dishes for the Plague-ridden

Any meal a plagued person may, in his good fortune, be given to eat may be his last meal, and so therefore, while there be some who will say waste not anything upon him, I advocate that meal should be of the best. I would counsel that you go out to snare a loon and give him leg of loon, boiled, with a little mashed turnip – than which, as I have writ before, there is no finer dish. That, or a dish of Mixed Knuckles (but afterward, still do remember to destruct the bowl from which he's eaten).

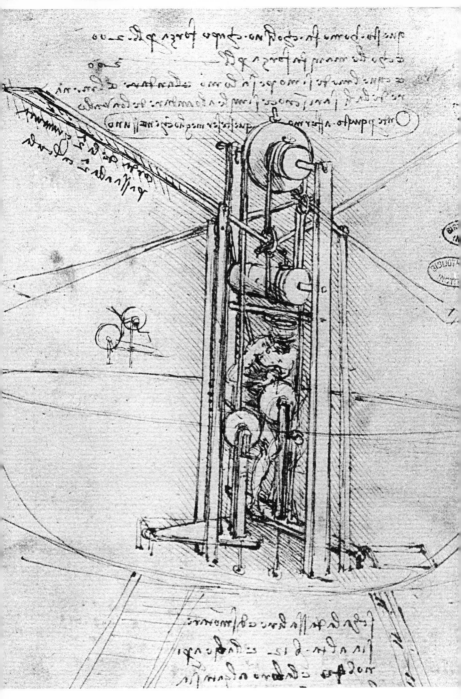

Leonardo's Giant Whisk had the disadvantage of being operated from within, its unfortunate driver being in constant
danger of drowning in the custard or whatever he was whisk-
ing.
MsB. fol. 8or.

My Simple Dishes

Here are some of the simple dishes I would set before My Lord Lodovico did I not but know he would reject them forthwith for their delicacy and purity and demand his mess of meat and bones instead:

❖ 6 BOILED SPROUTS and in their midst a pile of sturgeon's roe with custard.*

❖ A BOILED ONION of the medium size that rests upon a slice or slither of good buffalo cheese and surmounted by one black olive, quartered.

❖ ONE PLUM, stoned and quartered, then laid upon a thinnish slice of raw cow meat dried three months in the sun. Beside it, a sprig of apple blossom.

❖ ONE EGG of hen, hard-boiled, removed from its shell, and with its yolk scooped out and mixed with peppered pine-nuts before returning to its home.

❖ A YOUNG COW'S LIVER, finely pounded, and with some taste of sage and pepper in it. – This to go with bread or crusty porridge.

❖ SMALL SHRIMP AND SEA-HORSE lightly boiled then peeled and served with custard on them.

*The custard of these days was a savoury preparation the ingredients for which varied from locality to locality. In Florence it was made with flour, milk and mustard-seed. The 'Crema di Napoli' had a fish-base. In the north of Italy it numbered honey and vinegar amongst its ingredients. Any of these ways it seems hardly a suitable accompaniment to caviare.

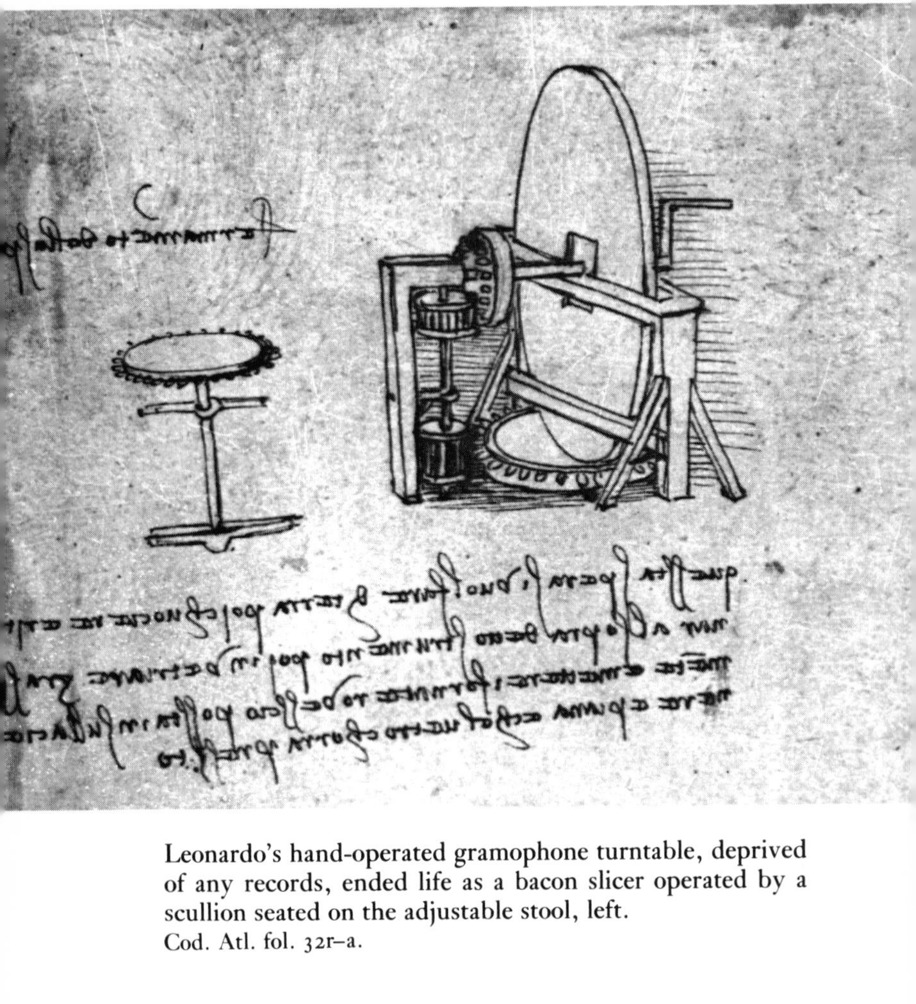

Leonardo's hand-operated gramophone turntable, deprived of any records, ended life as a bacon slicer operated by a scullion seated on the adjustable stool, left.
Cod. Atl. fol. 32r–a.

A DISH OF SPINACH boiled only, then chopped and on its top an egg but lightly poached out of its shell, around it all some further broken egg with cheese of buffalo.

THREE SLITHERS OF RAW CARROT each carved in the shape of a sea-horse with a caper on each and peck of anchovy sauce beside them.

❀ A THIN SLICE OF YOUNG COW-RUMP, no more than half the size of a hand, covered in a sauce of pounded tuna and cream, and with another thin slice of young cow-rump atop it – and this surmounted by a half-dozen sliced pickled cherries of Bergamo.

❀ A DISH OF BONES from the rib of a lamb, each with a little meat upon one end, lightly roasted, and a paper cap upon the other after cooling. This with a few leaves of mint atop.

❀ THE FINEST PIG-MEAT, boiled and finely pounded, then mixed with closely-grated apple and closely-grated carrot and a hen-egg and made into small balls that then are fried a golden brown and served upon a bed of rice and agro-dolce.

❀ which I call PIG WITH EGG and bread. Thin slithers off the back of pig that you have hung last winter each but the length of half a hand, and these are placed beneath the fire, but not to burn – three minutes only that does cook them. Or else you place the slithers in a pan but lightly smeared with oil and on the flames do place it – yet again for but three minutes, and then in that same fat two eggs of hen without their shells you keep until their albumens are white. And by the side of this fine dish, a hand-sized piece of bread cooked lightly in an olive oil with garlic added too and cooked until a golden brown.

❀ A HEN BOILED STUFFED WITH GRAPES, and with some carrots and an onion boiling there beside it; but then when cooked with just its breasts removed and served up tenderly with turnip pieces fried and peas.

❀ A BOWL OF THAT WHICH THAT SAME HEN WAS COOKED IN left unadulterated except a little salt or pepper.

The illustrated menu Leonardo and Botticelli produced for
their Trattoria – the drawing may show the hand of Botticelli
but the writing is unmistakably that of Leonardo. No one, let
alone customers or chefs, could make sense of it at all.
William Thomson Collection.

✿ which I called MIXED COW PIE.* From the rib of cow you cut the parts most tender next the bone and chop them into thumb-size bits; and mix these with the cow's own kidney chopped the same. Sprinkle flavourings upon them now – to suit your taste – and add some grated testicle for interest; and then you place the all within an earthen pot of stock of cow that covers every piece, and on its top you do prepare a roof of crusty porridge that is still soft. And now into the oven for such time as all the meats are cooked and porridge glorious brown. – Mashed turnip is the true companion to this dish.

*We have to admit to being a little puzzled by the rhythm of the writings of the longer recipes in this section (also by that for 'Shoulder of Serpent' – q.v.). The description of these particular dishes – which display as revolutionary an attitude toward mediaeval food as the Renaissance artists were showing toward the past in their works – is in a style of writing we have not come to associate with Leonardo. Therefore we have to ask, is this Leonardo's work – or some other's that he has copied, as so often was his wont? Without any doubt it could be his mind which was capable of thinking up such dishes – as new in his time as our own 'nouvelle cuisine' and concerning which we know he had experimented with earlier when Sandro Botticelli and he tried to run the 'Three Frogs' in Florence (see 'Gastronomic Life' p. 19).

In our opinion the most likely explanation concerning these recipes is that Leonardo had discussed his new ideas with one of the professional writers at Ludovico's Court, with Matteo Bandelli the novelist, with Bernardo Bellincioni the playwright, with Baldassare Taccone, Ludovico's Chancellor who wrote the 'Paradiso' play that Leonardo designed, or, most likely of all, with Platino Plato, the orator and poet with whom we know Leonardo was very close, and whose style these writings most closely resemble. And he (or one of the others), after listening to Leonardo talk, may have written down the recipes in his own words for Leonardo to copy out later.

And the other question we have to ask about some of these new dishes is 'but how were they eaten?' – bearing in mind that the pointed knife and the fingers were the normal table instruments of the time. No, we think that by the time of these recipes Leonardo must have come up with what must be considered one of his supreme creations, one of the great contributions of the Renaissance to civilization, the three-pronged fork. Otherwise, caviare with a pointed knife? Spinach and soft egg with the fingers?

❧ which I call BATTERED FISH WITH TURNIP FINGERS. It does you well to treat your turnips first in this fine dish. Boil them in a stock for as long as turnips take to turn tender-hard – but not yet soft. And then remove them from the pot and chop them into finger-lengths. And now, in this new guise, they must await their turn to cook again another way – the while you take some smallish fish the length of half an arm and tidy it but well. Now mix an egg without its shell into a paste of flavoured maize and with it coat this tidy fish. Meantime you have prepared a pan of sizzling oil upon the fire to welcome this said coated fish and give it hospitality the next part of a quarter hour. And when Sir Fish is from this pan removed you use it as a warm and tasty shelter for your turnip fingers until they go a golden brown. The two, the fish and golden turnip are perfect company (and sometimes there are those who will sprinkle on their tops a little salt and vinegar).

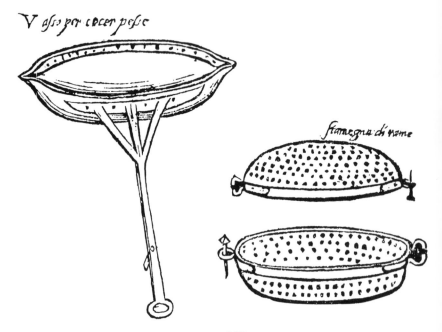

padella p fare oui friolate

❊ which I call TRANSFORMED FISH. You take a fish, a noble salmon from the sea, you gut it, scale it, poach it then you break it up removing every little bone and all impurity. And now the mystery of this dish; you mix this broken fish with beaten egg of hen and salt and pepper and mould it in your hands to make some fist-size balls or cakes which then you coat with crumbs of bread – a little albumen may help them stick – and place these coated broken fish inside a pan of burning oil until the heat and oil perform their skills and all is golden brown. – A sprig of parsley is the garnish for this simple dish.

On the Many and Curious Uses of the Cucumber

While a cucumber may be eaten raw (but without its skin and seed) and likewise stewed, there are those who still will use it as a decoration only, carving varied faces down its sides, and others yet that find more curious uses for it, like Elena Bastibari who was burnt at the stake for dalliance with one. For My Lord it is his favoured laxative, while My Lady Beatrice orders six each night and rubs the jelly round the seed upon her skin, and most of all her face, and to this she attributes her lustre that so many do remark upon. For me, a cucumber in brine is all I ask.

motaio

On the Improper Use of Blanc-manges

I do not feel that persons (who I do not know but yet have heard of) who claim that meat or poultry they have pounded then mixed with rice and honey and milk of almond have any right to call their dish 'blanc-mange'. To me a dish that's called 'blanc-mange' is also white but quivers to the touch and tastes but sweet and fishy. To its devising I will concern myself.

Porcupine

The meat of the porcupine tastes like that of the hedgehog. The people of the Po use it as a laxative, and also claim it is helpful against scabies and leprosy. Salted, it is helpful to those who suffer from night incontinence, as then it regulates the urine flux.

Bear

The cooking of bears is a subject I am not willing to discuss. Though let me advise all those with little hair upon their heads that bear fat, if rubbed upon their heads, will prevent further loss and even promote the growth of new hair.

On Unseemly Behaviours
at My Lord's Table

These are unseemly habits that a guest at My Lord's table should not contract – and this catalogue I base upon my observations this last year of those who did attend the table of My Lord:

No guest should sit upon the table, nor sit with his back toward the table, nor upon the lap of any other guest

Nor should he place his leg upon the table

Neither should he sit beneath the table for any length of time

He should not place his head upon his plate to eat

He should not take food from off his neighbour's plate unless first he asks consent

He should not place unpleasing or half-chewed pieces of his own food upon his neighbour's plate without first asking him

He should not wipe his knife upon his neighbour's clothing

Nor use his knife to carve upon the table

He should not clean his armour at the table

He should not take the food from off the table and place it in his purse or boot for later use

He should not take bites of fruit from off the fruit dish and then return the bitten fruits to that same dish

He should not spit in front of him

Nor yet beside him

He should not Pinch nor Slap his neighbour

He should not make Snorting Noises nor indulge in Nudging

He should not roll his eyes nor yet make fearful faces

He should not place his finger in his nose or ear while making conversation

He should not make models, nor light fires, nor practise tying knots upon the table (unless My Lord requests him so)

He should not set loose his birds upon the table

Nor snakes nor beetles either

He should not play upon his lute, or any other instrument which might be to his neighbour's detriment (unless My Lord requests him so)

He should not sing nor make a speech nor shout abuse nor yet tell ribald riddles if a lady is beside him

He should not Plot at table (unless it's with My Lord)

He should not make lewd suggestions to the pages of My Lord nor trifle with their bodies

Nor should he set alight his neighbour while at table

He should not strike a serving person (unless it be in self-defence)

And if he is to vomit then he leaves the table

Likewise if he's to urinate

Remains*

If the foods which have survived a feast look too good to feed to the dogs and servants (whose sensibilities might be offended by unaccustomed shapes, and digestions suffer from unaccustomed richnesses), then they can be cut up and placed in a pot with a mixture of nine parts porridge and water and lightly boiled for half a day to remove the garish nature of their tastes. Then they can be proferred to all creatures who will only be the more grateful to you for your trouble and thoughtfulness.

*This passage occurs almost word for word in the long letter Niccòlo Macchiavelli wrote to Cosimo de Medici (Archivi di Stato, Florence) at the time he and Leonardo were in the employ of the Borgias in Rome in 1504. While there can be no certain proof of the original authorship we have to bear in mind the tone of the passage and also Leonardo's habit of copying other people's works into his Note Books.

On Wine

I have heard it said that those who do not use wine in moderation become tired, shaking, pale, smelling, bleary-eyed, sterile, impotent, forgetful, bald and old before their time. Judging from the appearance of my friend Gaudio this is all true.

Fried Flowers

There is but one to my certain knowledge you may use and that is the blossom of the marrow. Coat it with a light batter and fry it quickly in your oil-pan.

Cabbage Jam

Wipe the cabbage perfectly dry and remove all that moves from within its leaves. Chop all of it to the size of ducats. Place it in a pan with half its weight in honey, some sprigs of marjoram and some bay leaves. Place this in a pan by the side of a fire, its top covered with a cloth so the smoke does not intrude into it and when it starts to steam place it more over the fire, and let the jam boil until it is reduced to one third its original mass (taking care all the while to keep it well skimmed and stirred with a wooden ladle). Pour it into pots you should cover with leaves of rhubarb. Battista claims this is an ideal accompaniment to bad cow or dead sheep, imbuing both fleshes with a totally acceptable taste. To me it seems totally unnecessary company for two dishes which are unnecessary in the first place. I shall have none of it.

Items

Eggs blessed by the priest taste like any other eggs

A person of Breeding does not blow his nose upon the table-cloth

Pickled Donkey with Prunes

A Menu for Three Uncivil Fellows

Who these days eats Pig-berries and Quangle-berries ?

Frog and Kidney Pie

A Dish for Buffoons, Itinerant Singers, Ne'er-do-wells, Hooligans, Spendthrifts, Boobies and Babblers.

What else should it be called for persons who are sensitive – a dish which is but Smoked Bowels of Pig ? Likewise a Boiled Calf's Udder ?

A Carver* proves his worth if he can carve an egg up in the air they say. Yet how shall this ability help him with the hen ?

*Carvers, like assassins, formed one of the most powerful groups of persons in fifteenth-century Italy, in very great demand, booked months ahead, paid enormous sums for the demonstration of their skills. Leonardo in his lost Treatise on Carving *is said to have held them in very great respect.*

126

The Serving of Snails

After you have boiled your snails in the sprout-water then place them on a plate you have made of hardened porridge smeared with honey and with indentations in the plate into which the shells may fit. Now, you bring down your hammer upon each, and the broken shell-pieces will stick to the honey and thus you can more tidily removed the snail from their midst before dipping it with your fingers into the sauce of buttered garlic and parsley-flower.

– But if there is no way to entice a dead snail out of its shell except with the hammer then I suspect this cannot be a dish suited to Princes or Princesses of sensitivity. I suspect – no, I am convinced of it – that there must be some more tidy way to eat the dish and I shall apply myself to find it.

Snail Soup

Smash the shells of 24 snails and remove what is edible from the mess. Place, with a lettuce, half a calves head, some parsley-flower and garlic in a boiling pan for three hours. Pour through your sieve into the serving bowl.

On the Eating Habits
of some Others I have Met
in High Places

ITEM: My Lord Cesare Borgia has so many Tasters in his entourage his foods turn cold while they are tasting them. I do doubt that he has ever known a dish that's even warm.

ITEM: Sir Maximilian Sforza it is impossible to place at table except near an open door as he does never change his body linen and then when he does eat he has the very dirty habit of letting out his ferrets on the table to nibble other people's foods.

ITEM: His Holiness in Lent eats little with a pious look upon his face but then he leaves the table early and journeys to that other table that he keeps within his private quarters (complete with kitchen, cooks and good foods too) and there he fills himself with capon, quail and coot.

ITEM: his sister's son the Cardinal Salviati, has the habit at the Lenten table of being served a plate of beans apart saying he cannot eat the beans that others eat with oil and must have his with gentle butter (and yet he is a Tuscan man, brought up on beans in oil). Truth is, it is not beans upon this plate he has, but testicles of chicken – so much for the great sacrifice our Cardinal of Florence does make in Lent.

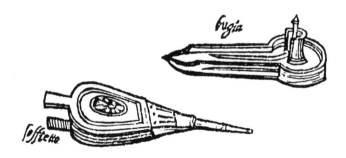

ITEM : His Holiness permits – but not in Lent – the priests who eat at lower tables to throw their chickens and their soups at all who visit the said tables and dance upon the table tops and punch those who do not join them in their faces.

ITEM : My Lady Beatrice has the sweetest habits, with white gloves upon her hands that she changes thrice a meal, and I wish that all were just like her.

On Eating Artichokes

My Lord Lodovico tells me I am to devise a way whereby to eat artichokes without spitting out on to the table nine-tenths of what one places in one's mouth. The way is simple. The leaves are cut from the fruit before the meal – leaving just the base of artichoke, all of which is edible and none of which has need of spitting.

Butter Lamb

Using butter which has been rendered very firm by being left in iced water make a model of a lamb one arm high upon a board. Return to the pool of ice water.

Bee Pie

Stew fourteen frogs in a pig's bladder for some hours. Debone the legs of frog and cut into small pieces. Mix with a little sweet woodruff, some honey and all of one hen-egg and mould into the shape of a bee.

Anchovy Soup

Boil your anchovies – but instead of in water place them in a pot with many slices of water melon – which will to some small extent detract from the saltiness of the fish, and also a little agrodolce will help in this battle. Then, as the juices of the melons are consumed, add fresh melons and continue doing so for half a day. And then you may add breadcrumbs to thicken the surviving liquid and after a while remove it from the pot and drain it through your sieve. The dish, though a great favourite of Guiano Mattesi* and his cronies, is in my opinion ready only to be poured back into the ocean – and then no doubt to the detriment of those unfortunates who live in it. Also, the stink from its preparation, and which permeates every stone of the building for many days, is such that in the past I have removed myself to Veregano** to escape from it.

*Guiano Mattesi, a celebrated dwarf of the time, a great favourite of Ludovico's, actor and singer in many of the spectacles Leonardo prepared for Ludovico.

**The Palazzo Ducale at Vigevano, some 30kms south-west of Milan was a favourite country retreat of Ludovico's, and more especially of his wife Beatrice. When Leonardo was in especial disfavour at the Court in Milan – through the failure of one of his many schemes in the Castello – Ludovico would encourage him (with some authority) to visit there for a period and paint ceilings – some very slight vestiges of the designs which Leonardo made are still visible. So, Leonardo may not be being strictly truthful here when he ascribes his absences in Vigevano as ordered by his allergy toward the preparation of this soup.

Three More Simple Soups

1 SOUP OF CHESTNUTS

You must hammer and crack your chestnuts and boil them in a plain water first. Then after a while you remove them from the water and peel off any of the skins still upon them, then boil them gently for a longer while in a hen-stock until they are soft enough to be passed easily through your horse-sieve. Now heat this up with some oil and honey, some salt and pepper, decorate with some little leaves, and there is your soup of chestnuts. It is good against the after-effects of wild spider bites, and also for sticking together the pages of books.

2 SOUP OF GRAPES

Boil together as many grapes as you can spare – they need no added waters for they contain their own. Then pass them through your horse-sieve, beat some eggs into this and add some honey and there is your soup of grapes. My friend Gaudio Sporgere says the dish is a waste and he will not permit his grapes to be used thus.

3 SOUP OF LITTLE PEAS

Only little peas should be used in the making of this soup, and also you must use all of the pea, both the inside and outside of the pod. Boil a basket of them in a pig-stock and strain through your horse-sieve, add some pepper and salt and mint, and there is your soup of little peas which I, not liking little peas, find very dull indeed.

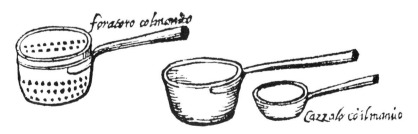

For Salai to Get

Candles
Frog food
Fresh pigskin for my drums
More of the red wine of Mantua

To Remove Blood from the Tablecloth

Blood on a table-cloth – which may be pursuant to an accident with the carving knife or an assassination – need cause little worry, nor need the company be disturbed by removal of the whole cloth as in olden times – if the affected part is treated immediately with vigorous rubbings of warm sprout-water.

A List of Lenten Mortification Dishes

𝕻igs-blood 𝕻udding
𝕸ushrooms served on their backs
𝕭urnt 𝕻orridge

𝕴 shall recollect more another time.

On Appointing a New Taster

My Lord advertises for a new Taster and those who hear his appeal, to them it can mean but one thing only: the old Taster has done his job too well.* But it is not against the artificial poisons that he might find admitted to his foods My Lord has need of any Taster for, but against the poisoners in his kitchens, those so-called cooks who serve him putrefying fleshes and decomposing fruits. These are what killed Sergo Canallati, such tastes as I have known and been disturbed by these last two year. Were My Lord to put his kitchens well in order he'd have no need of any Taster at his table.

On Liquorice

Over-indulgence in liquorice can be harmful to persons with gallstones or who have trouble in passing water – I base my observation upon the condition of my foul-smelling friend Gaudio Fullente who is at all times with a piece of liquorice in his mouth and who suffers from these faults. But I may be wrong and it may turn out to be the saffron he adds to his wine which aggravates his condition.

*Leonardo is incorrect in assuming this. Ludovico Sforza, with a duplicity one associates with the Borgias rather than the Sforzas had himself arranged for poison to be administered to the dishes that his Taster Sergio Canallati had to eat in order that he, Sergio, should die and so could be replaced by one Gentio Ciccania, a celebrated poisoner of the time, whose task it became as the new Taster at Court – and under Ludovico's direction – to administer slow doses of poison to the dishes served to Ludovico's ineffectual elder brother Giuliano, the Duke of Milan, so that Ludovico, upon his brother's death, could assume the title. But obviously Leonardo was not privy to this scheme.

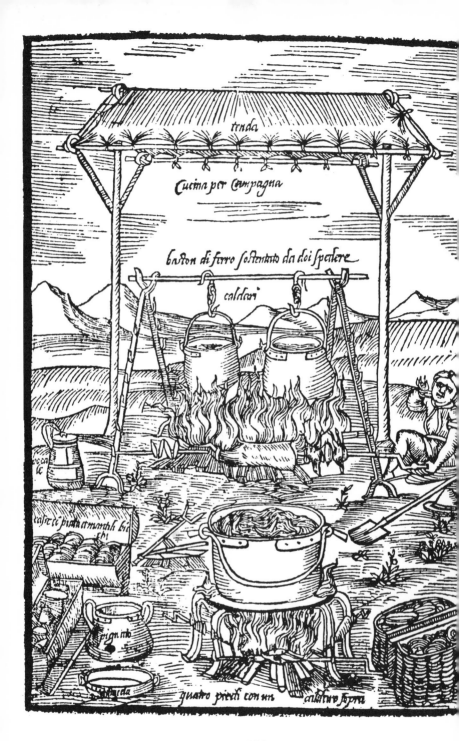

134

neuauejifa

On the Parts of a Pig

There is no part of a pig which may not be consumed except
for two. His blood may be dried in the sun to make a sausage.
His bones boiled in waters with garlics and peppers make a
pig soup. His skin may be melted down to make into fats. All
his fleshes may be cooked and used for themselves or for a Pig
Pie, and all parts of his head may be cooked, that is save for
two for not once have I heard of a pig's eyes making any dish.
(Salai will try them for me.) So I say that of all animals a pig is
of man his best friend.

A Thought

Would porridge balls in gold-leaf attract My Lord's digestion ?

Further on Lenten Mortification Dishes

At times of Fast it is not enough that dish should just *look* sad, it must *taste* sad, too. And what sadder sight and taste combined is there than that of yesterday's cold porridge cooked without an added flavouring ?

Observations upon Vegetables

❖ ASPARAGUS ❖

These sticks when boiled and dressed with salt, oil and pepper, will make your eyes shine, will eliminate swollen stomach and other internal disturbances, will remove pains from your back and thighs, and act as a gentle laxative. Though do not over-indulge in asparagus sticks because that could cause ulcers of the bladder. And always keep a little juice of crushed asparagus on hand to offer any guests at your table who might complain of being poisoned.

❖ CARROTS ❖

These are best cooked under the ashes of the fire, then cleaned, peeled, and cut into cubes which are dressed with oil, vinegar, a little warm wine and sweet herbs or honey. There is little nutrient in them but they are useful for calming billiosness and decorating a plain porridge.

❀ PARSNIPS ❀

These are in reality sweet white carrots which may be boiled (together with some lettuce or other greens) and then dressed with salt, vinegar and coriander (in which event they are believed to have great aphrodisiacal qualities); or else fried in oil after their skins are scraped off (after they have been boiled) and after they have been sprinkled with a fine flour (in which case they are looked upon as effective against pleurisy and dropsy – though take care never to use ancient parsnips for they have it in their roots to cause vertigo and falling down).

In Puglia the juice of parsnips mixed with a little crushed hops is drunk as a wine, but they say it causes frequent delirium.

In Puglia also they have a way of cooking parsnips whereby they are boiled in water before being thrown away and a second lot of peeled parsnips is added to the same water and boiled in it.

❀ LETTUCE ❀

Lettuce, because of its high moisture content, gives you an appetite for other foods, and therefore should not be offered at the start of a meal unless your larder is well-stocked. Some lettuces when cooked in oil prove good for calming a cough and may also be used as a laxative – but if taken in too large quantities, or too frequently, can be harmful to the eyesight.

My cook Battista is fond of serving me with unwashed lettuce in a brown broth which has a lemon flavour. I fear I am not fond of it and this I normally give to my dog if I can without Battista seeing me.

The milk which gushes out of a lettuce when you wound it in the main stem is very conducive to a peaceful sleep if enough is obtained to soak on a little bread, though they do say that if emptied into rivers or the sea it can cause the fish to die.

137

❖ GOAT'S BEARD ❖
(*or Endive*)

Battista uses these to decorate her trifles. They are quite bitter to the taste and should be discarded from the plate immediately Battista leaves the room.

With the leaves and roots chopped together you can make a paste that is effective against bee-stings and scorpion bites.

❖ CAPERS ❖

These should never be boiled, just placed in a pan of hot water until the salty taste has disappeared. Then you put them in fresh cold water until they have cooled, and dress with a little oil and vinegar. Eaten in quantity they are a strong aphrodisiac, and also get rid of worms and prevent paralysis – though the people of Puglia, from whence come the best capers, claim that eaten with too great regularity, that causes the eater to vomit all day long.

❖ MALLOW ❖

This is one of the most useful of all vegetables. You can cook the leaves like you would spinnach. (The leaves uncooked are an antidote for wasps and spider-rates). You can cook the stalks like you would asparagus sticks. And you can eat the flowers, dipped in egg and fried, like you would the flowers of a marrow (they are especially effective against Swelling).

Battista says that to drink the juice of the mallow protects you from billiosness and other symptoms that led to her husband's madness.

❖ WILD CHICORY ❖

It is not advisable to eat this after cherries or prunes. The two do not mix happily and will cause sounds as of thunder to issue from your body.

A little, grated with mint then sprinkled on porridge, is used against running-nose and watering eyes in Lombardy.

❀ HOPS ❀

It is better for you to eat these boiled than fried, and even though they taste of very little they will help your blood and give you a vivacious colour.

Poached eggs without their shells make a good accompaniment to boiled hops.

❀ BUGROSSA ❀

This is what the Greeks used to call *porcellana*. It is very purifying for the blood if eaten uncooked; while cooked with honey and water it will get rid of ulcers in the mouth and melancholy.

❀ RADICCHIO ❀

The roots of this when grated and dressed with salt, oil and vinegar act as an aphrodisiac, and are also good for Nauseous Mouth, Intoxication, Contagious Diseases and Suffering.

❀ PRIMROSES ❀

Primrose leaves are very appetising but not very digestible. Boiled, they are good for stones in the bladder.

❀ PORCELLANA ❀

This is what the Greeks used to call *bugrossa*. You chop the stems very finely and mix them with finely chopped onions and dress with salt, oil, vinegar and sometimes pepper and cinnamon, and then sprinkle on your porridge. If you eat it too often it will adversely affect your eyesight and your sexuality, but will be food for your gout.

❀ ACETOSA ❀

Uncooked it is very good for calming rage. Boiled, it helps against scabies and itching.

More Dishes for Poor People

1 Porridge with One Herb. – Mix into the porridge a little tansywort.

2 Porridge with Two Herbs. – Mix into the porridge a little tansywort and dried sambuca flowers.

3 This, for Festivals and special occasions, Porridge with Three Herbs. – Mix with the porridge a little tansywort, some dried sambuca flowers, and the juice of red poppies.

Frog in a Box

A frog may be hung up and dried in the sun and after a period of time when it is black its legs may be eaten. But if I was to place a dead frog, or even the legs of a dead frog, in a box full of goose-fat, and with all air removed from it, and seal the box and not open it for twelve months, would that dead frog still be worthy of eating? But what if I should not have a box-opener, how then could I tell? – The prudent man hangs up his dead frog in the sun.

On the Properties of Lettuce

Lettuce is the enemy of sleeplessness. If consumed uncooked and in quantities before retiring it will guarantee repose. I myself at the end of a tiring day boil large quantities of it in order to extract their juices which I then drink to produce an undisturbed sleep.

The Sausage of Leo X

These are the instructions of Fabrizio Menaeus, cook to His Holiness. For each person's sausage you pass the brains of a cow through a sieve and mix with a little milk. Now you take the bones out of a chicken, a pheasant and a partridge and grind up the meat twice until very fine. Mix it with the milked brains, some flour, an egg, and very finely chopped-up black truffle. Now, on some paper sprinkled with flour, mould it into the shape of a sausage one metre long and leave it to lie on a marble slab for a day and a night. And then cook it in pig fat and serve with a bunch of carnations.

As I have said this is the recipe for each person's sausage, but when I have eaten at His Holiness's table, His Holiness's sausage has been twice as vast as mine and that of any other's.

Cooking with Poisons

Now I am to meet with My Lord Cesare and Maestro Macchiavelli to discuss my knowledge of poisons – and that is slight,* Salai being so reluctant to co-operate with me on my experiments ever since he discovered me and did object so to my placing gradually increasing amounts of strychnine and belladonna in his morning porridge, and was loathe to accept my explanation that it was but to build up his immunity to the substances should they be proferred him from other less friendly sources – bearing in mind the reputation of our good host's household.

I am clear on some matters though. The choice of poison must depend upon the effect you are trying to create with your subject. Thus, this one causes Sneezing, this one Itching, this one Jumping and Convulsions, and this one Total

---

*Although in other writings Leonardo makes many references to animals curing themselves of poisons, and also (in Codex Atlanticus 346v.a) comes up with the ingenious plan for putting out of action the crew of an enemy boat by shooting on to them a poison of 'arsenic mixed with venom of toad, saliva of mad dog and dogwood berries'. But whether this was to be administered in a liquid or powder form Leonardo does not state.

Death. Nor should the different poisons available be ever confused by one initiating himself into the poisoner's craft. He must learn that Strychnine causes Stiff Neck and Terror; that the brown and black berries of the deadly nightshade cause Wild Eyes and Deliriousness; that Monkshood (which is so often mistook for the roots of the horse-radish) brings on Tingling and Vomitting; and that Hemlock is one that causes Total Death.

There are others the effects of which I am uncertain through Salai's selfishness; and these include Snakeroot, Rhubarb, Tansy, Black Baneberries, Henbaneberries, Mistletoe, Jerusalem Artichokes, and the mold of certain cheeses of Mantua. Though of one other matter I am certain. A good poison should always be administered at the beginning of a meal, for it works quickest on an empty stomach, and so used is both beneficial to the poisoner who need not use more than a small measure of his weapon, and to the Host who will not wish the subsequent Revels he will have planned for his guests to be disturbed by his Victim's agony.

Tasks for Salai

Clear up the messes he has made
Feed my favourite frogs
Keep Galtieri away from me unless he is bringing me monies
Mend the leg of my writing bench he has broken
Desist from clicking his knuckles when bored

On Bread and Meat

I have been thinking of taking a piece of bread and placing it between two pieces of meat. But what should I call such a dish?

Snail Soup

If using snails that have been deliberately fattened in an enclosure and fed with parsley leaves and the soup of vegetables, then these snails may be cooked after but three days of starvation – for any scums and slime left in them after that time will be pure scum and slime and not harmful to whosoever eats it.

But if using wild snails that have been collected in the countryside it is necessary to starve these snails for two whole weeks before the pot reaps them – as the scums and slime in them, being oft the product of poisons in plants eaten by the snails yet not affecting them adversely could yet be highly harmful to humans – as, they say, was how the Duke Giulio Orsini met his end at table in Mantua – thus these scums and slime need completely to be eradicated.

Then after this starvation, the snails being weak from hunger and many in a state of unconsciousness, will feel little of the cunning pin that coaxes them from their homes, nor the hammer blows that break their shells should that be the method by which they are to be evacuated.

Now should they be soaked in soft water (to which an anchovy has been added) for six hours, and washed again under more soft running water to clean off all the last vestiges of scums and slime.

And now they may be cooked (there are some who prefer to cut off the black parts of the snail's tail – for it has a bitter taste). Place the snails in a boiling pot, adding some few flavourings, a handful of herbiage leaves, some sprouts, an anchovy, a little cut dill, a small calf's head – this amount of flavouring to every hundred snails. Let the pot boil over the fire for ten minutes at a steady pace, then move it further from the fire that it may simmer for some six or seven hours. Let it cool then drain it through a coarse hair bag. The resultant broth should be served cold with lumps of broken porridge in it, and the waste be safely given to the dogs.

On Bread and Meat (II)

I have been thinking amore of the bread and the meat. What if I were to place the meat between the two pieces of bread ? And what should I call that dish?

More on Blanc-manges

Should it prove difficult and even dangerous to eat my new blanc-mange with knives – as I predict – I would provide each sitting with a spoon. But if I were to ask My Lord for spoons for every one I fear his Treasury would tell him he can't afford the Gold. So I fear that those who wish to taste my good blanc-mange with knives alone will know a multitude of spills and bloody injuries. – *Or else they can refrain.*

On an Aid to the Digestion

I am wondering if between dishes at My Lord's table – and especially if those dishes are not of the first order – instead of the appearance of tumblers and dwarves, the performance of some licentious women dancers would not be a better aid to the digestion.

On Coelius Apicius

I have been re-reading *De re Culinaria* by Coelius Apicius. The man was a fool. Who to-day would want to eat dormice in honey, or the tongues of storks and cranes, or leeks stewed in honey then coated with the entrails of tuna?

On the Correct Seating
of the Assassin at Table

If there is an assassination planned for the meal then it is seemliest that the assassin should be seated next to he who is to become the subject of his craft (whether upon that person's left or on his right must depend upon the method of the assassin) as this will cause less interruption to the conversation if the action of the event is confined to one small area. Indeed, the fame of Ambroglio Descarte, the foremost assassin of My Lord Cesare Borgia, rests greatly on his ability to perform his task without a single member of the table noticing let alone being inconvenienced by his actions.

After the corpse (and the bloodstains if any) are removed by the serving persons, it is customary for the assassin also to withdraw from the table as his presence may sometimes be disturbing to the digestions of the persons who now find themselves seated next to him, and to this end a good host will always have a fresh guest, who will have waited without, ready to join the table at this juncture.

Stuffed Dormouse

This is the manner in which it was done in ancient times: it was stuffed with pepper, nuts and sprouts; sewn up; covered with honey and poppy seed; and cooked over the fire. But now Salai tells me eating dormice is wrong, and instead gives me a chicken again. How he bores me, and the chicken.

On the Character of
Goffredo Giuliani

Goffredo Giuliani* is a shallow dolt and lying toad, not fit even for the company of Umbrian swine or the diseased sheep of Padua. I wash my hands of him. His breath is foul though not so stinking as his clothes.

*The reason for this rare outburst of Leonardo's, unlike any other words he ever penned (except in relation to his lackadaisical pupil Salai) is not difficult to understand. Giuliani was the inefficient Master of Water-works at the Castello in Milan, in charge of implementing Leonardo's designs first for the new kitchens – which were such a disaster (see details p. 40), then for the new bathroom for Ludovico's private apartments that Leonardo was made to design. After three months of slow work on this room Ludovico, impatient for the new bathing experience Leonardo had promised him, decided to try it, but unfortunately at a time while Leonardo was absent visiting his friend Luca Pacioli the mathematician at Pavia and had not had occasion to test it for himself. Everything that could have gone wrong went wrong. Ludovico with two pages went inside the room (20ft by 20ft and all bath), operated the levers which hydraulically closed the doors and started the ceiling-high waterfalls – one warm, one cold – which were the main sources of water. Once bathed, Ludovico pulled the lever which was meant to drain away the waters – but to no effect except that more and more water now started pouring in, directed from 100 nozzles Leonardo had set – jacuzzi-like – into the side walls. And the lever meant to open the doors of the room also failed to work. The screams of Ludovico, now supported by his pages on the rapidly rising surface of the waters, went unheard outside the room, drowned by the water-operated accordions and drums sets Leonardo had installed for his master's pleasure, and the first that anyone else in the Castello knew that anything was wrong was when the west wall of the room collapsed outward under the pressure of the water within, releasing an avalanche of bath water – and Ludovico with his pages – into his mother's new apartments beneath.
  When Leonardo subsequently returned from Pavia he went to investigate and then found Giuliani had fitted no proper drainage system to lead the waters away. But this was no excuse to Ludovico who dispatched him to

boccale

On the Medical Properties of some Herbs

❀ ANISEED gives your breath an interesting smell, and the strength of its vapours will help to cure your headache.

❀ CUMIN which gives you a pale face, may be taken safely in porridge or on its own by widow-women wishing to feign desolation in the months after their husband's decease. Also effective against dysentry.

❀ MINT is good for increasing sexual interest and for rekindling lost sexual vigour. For these reasons the military leaders of ancient days forbade it to their soldiers when engaged on foreign campaigns – so they would stay chaste and thus be better fighters. Also effective against rabid dog-bites.

❀ POPPIES. The stems of the white poppy when chopped up and drunk with wine is what the physicians give to persons suffering from elephantisis. It reduces both their size and their suffering.

The juice of red poppies is what they recommend to persons suffering from excessive anxiety, and also what they prescribe to persons suffering from insomnia.

Vigevano to paint ceilings for a month. So it would seem reasonable to deduce that it was from this time that Leonardo wrote his curt observations upon the character of Goffredo Giuliani.

❧ CORIANDER – its seeds mixed with honey and grape juice, or with vinegar and sugar, act to combat the unsavoury vapours that go to the head of persons addicted to too large quantities of wine.

I hear that one coriander seed chopped up and drunk by a woman will stop her menstrual period for one day, and two seeds for two days, and so on.

❧ CELERY. Its stalks should be eaten by a person who suspects he is being poisoned by his wife. (But they are of little consequence against the bites of snakes.)

❧ THYME. A cloth soaked in thyme which has been cooked in vinegar and which you have then placed over your temple will cure your headache.

❧ SAGE is good for paralysis and helpful against snake-bites. It also helps to preserve your teeth when rubbed on them.

❧ MYRTLE. The effect of small sprigs of myrtle left to soak in a bowl of vinegar is very restorative to persons who are tired after heavy working – they should sit by it, not drink it for their restoration to be complete.

Also, a crown of myrtle sprigs worn on the head proves a protection against both intense heat and intense cold, and if you have not enough for a crown then two sprigs worn behind the ears will also prove effective.

Also, the odour of the myrtle sprigs when burnt is said to be displeasing to fleas and to cause them to disappear.

❀ BASIL. An excess of this is bad for one's stomach, harmful to one's eyesight, dangerous to one's liver, and in time likely to induce madness.

However, a small quantity used in wine and vinegar is quite useful against scorpion bites (though if you yourself have been chewing basil before you are bitten by a scorpion there is no way you can save yourself).

❀ RUGETTA. This hot grass when eaten with lettuce leaves stimulates sexuality in an incredible way. Cooked in water with broken bones it is also very effective against scorpion bites.

❀ HORSE-RADISH. Although by nature hot like rugetta it nevertheless, according to my friend Paulo Mordecani, has negative results so far as sexuality is concerned. Taken in moderation it acts as a purge to the intestines and can be rubbed on the head to relieve itching.

❀ DILL. Paulo Mordecani tells me that he drinks three cups of dill boiled in water to calm his wind, and that simply to smell boiled dill seeds will cure the hiccups.

❀ RUE. If it is rue that has been growing around a fig tree – which is the best rue – then it is a great friend of your stomach and may be used as a laxative. Other rue which does not grow around fig-trees may be used to give solace to persons bitten by spiders.

❀ THYME. Taken liberally with food is very good for clearing up cloudy vision; eaten chopped with honey it loosens catarrh; mixed with porridge proves an effective cure for sciatica; and when sprinkled on the floor it keeps vermin at a distance.

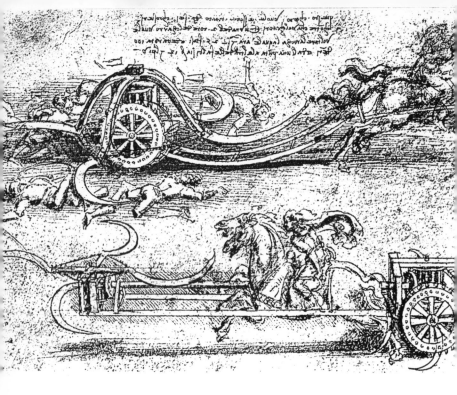

Leonardo's design for a giant watercress cutter was later made in his workshops at the Sforza Palace in Milan; but at its demonstration in the watercress fields outside the Palace it ran out of hand and killed sixteen members of the kitchen staff and three gardeners. Subsequently Ludovico used it with great effect against the French invading troops.
MsB. fol. 10r.

❀ OREGANO. Taken with hot water calms stomach cramps and alleviates indigestion. Added to wine combats the poison of spiders and scorpions.

❀ CATMINT. Its hotness makes it one of the most effective of herbs. It loosens and purges phlegm in the head and chest, mollifies the liver, softens the spleen, and helps to expel stones. Can also be used to keep snakes away.

150

�֎ MARJORAM. Boiled in water and sniffed it liberates the nostrils thus making you forget gluttonous urges. Chopped in vinegar and fat it may be spread on scorpion bites.

✿ CHERVIL. Chopped and drunk with wine it alleviates pains in the flanks; mixed with vinegar it loosens catarrh, expels tapeworms and destroys vermin; mixed with beeswax and fat it may be spread on the upper neck to alleviate earache.

✿ WATERCRESS. Very effective against stinging insects like bees and wasps. Also good for headaches, nausea, hiccups and dysentry.

✿ HAREHOUND. The seeds and chopped leaves of this very bitter herb are effective against snakes, chest and flank pains. Mixed with porridge and fried in oil it makes a very healthy first dish for babies, and gets rid of vermin.

✿ HYSSOP. Chopped and cooked in oil it will cure itchiness caused by parasite bites. Mixed with figs, honey, salt and cumin it removes stomach aches. Eaten on its own highly dangerous.

✿ PARSLEY. The seeds are effective against dysentry. Infused with sugared wine its leaves become a diuretic. Its roots cooked in wine will rid you of gall-stones, back-ache and aches of the flank. The herb is also an enemy of scorpions, and may be used as a potion to be spread of rabid dog-bites. My friend Paulo Mordecani says its effect on sexuality is negative.

Uncooked Chicken
(*Pollo sensa farina*)

Stuff a dead chicken with as many cut lemons as its cavity
will hold, then immerse it for 48 hours in your vinegar jar. I
am told it does taste well at the end of this time but may be
tough at the ends.

Roman Prune and Cauliflower Soup

Place a cauliflower in gently boiling water. After fifteen
minutes throw the water away and place the cauliflower in a
fatty broth for thirty minutes. At the end of that time throw
the cauliflower away and add a handful of stoned prunes and
cook for another thirty minutes. Remove the prunes and
serve. This dish does not taste very good, nor is it very good
for the stomach, the head, or persons with gall-stones.

Shepherd's Pie (I)

This is a dish I know is eaten by those who labour in the fields and others who work on the mountainsides and which they carry from their homes in the morning and sustains them throughout the day.

A flat porridge is baked and cut into pieces (10×20 cms). A slit is made in each to turn it into an envelope or pouch, this pouch then being filled with a mixture of diced prunes, grated chestnuts, powdered almond nuts and parts of a pig cooked and then mixed with an equal quantity of goat cheese.

I have many times thought of the advantage of this dish which enables one to feed substantially with the one hand while continuing to labour with the other.

Shepherd's Pie (II)

Take three shepherds, cleanse them thoroughly, then let them in your kitchens to choose which of your herbs their sheep do eat the most amongst their grasses. Now pound these herbs most thoroughly into a paste with oil and spread all on the sheep – with utmost generosity – that now you cook within a porridge crust inside your oven doors. This dish is so-called because, thanks to goodly shepherds, what's within the sheep's without as well and thus there is no conflict of its taste.

(This is the recipe of my friend Lucca Luciano)

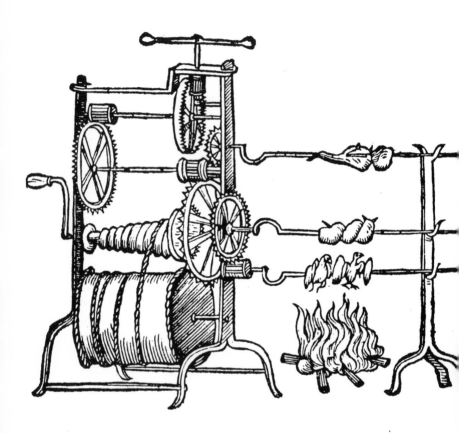

Molinello con tre ſpedi, che ſi volta da ſe, per forza de ruota, col tempo, a
foggia di Orologgio, come nella preſente Figura ſi diſmoſtra.

Cow Pattie

This is similar to a Shepherd's Pie except only the Parts of a Cow – bound together with Goat Cheese – are placed in the porridge pouch.

Bread and Ox-cheeks (I)

Bone and boil some ox-cheeks in waters which have previously held parsnips (this gives a very delicious taste to all the soft parts of an animal). When they are boiled very tender pass them through your mangle a number of times to make them as fine as possible – they should double their area in this process. Now place a piece of bread between these two cheek slices and serve with pickled nasturtiums.

Bread and Ox-cheeks (II)

I am debating if it would not be advisable to place the slice of ox-cheek between two pieces of bread rather than the other way round. This would create a dish the like of which has never been known on My Lord Lodovico's table. Indeed, one could place any variety of matter between the breads – udders, testicles, livers, ears, tails, every suchlike. And each content not being visible to the diner would be a veritable surprise when he attacked it with his knife. What should I call such a dish? *Bread Surprise.* *(to page 158)*

Leonardo's original 'spaghetti', made from coarse flours and rain water, was vast in concept, the strands over three feet in diameter, and endless in length. It was designed to feed armies, but the mechanisms for making it and the ground cow

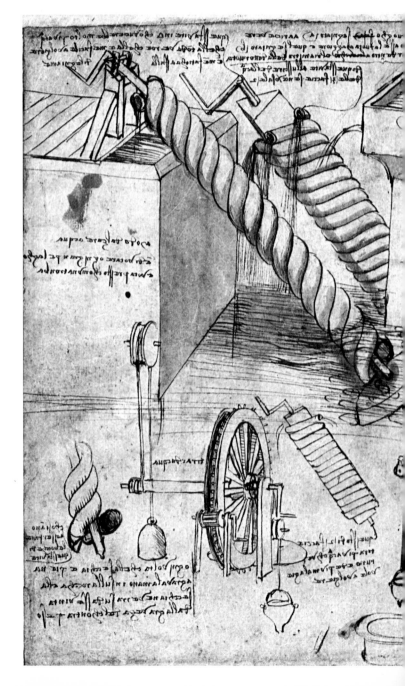

with basil sauce which was meant to accompany it, were so un-
wieldy in size that Cesare Borgia claimed only an army besieg-
ed in vast kitchens would have the resources to make use of it.
Cod. Atl. fol. v–a.

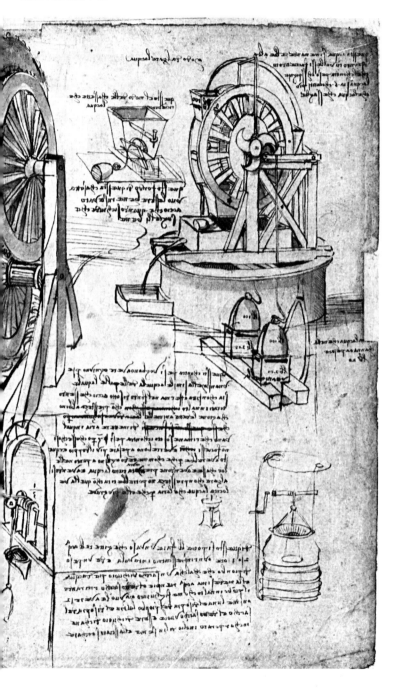

Gaudio's Smoky Sicilian Soup

Make a dough of flour, yolk of egg and rosewater and cut it into long worm-thick strips which you must further roll or pass through your mangle. Leave these strips to dry in the sun for two to three years then place them in a fatty broth with grated cheese and sweet flavourings, and a little saffron to colour it. Cook over a charcoal fire without any wet cloth over the top of the pot so that it acquires a smoky taste. – It is Gaudio's wont to add a bottle of strong wine to his portion of soup, but I cannot advise this to others as it causes Gaudio to produce wind and often to fall asleep at the table.

Mock Dormice

Should your dish require dormice, and should your larder be bare of them, you may squash and mould old figs to resemble the little creatures, creating their facial features with the aid of thistle-tops and scrapings of black truffle.

On the Dual Properties of Lemons

Lemons which have been used in the flavouring of cabbage leaves and other such insipids may be hung on old or unused garments and will help to preserve them by keeping away moths and other predators. But the lemons themselves, if not replaced from time to time, do deteriorate into a mould breeding parasities that can have a more dire effect upon the garments than any moth.

Cow Pastilles

The method of the Priors of S. Angelo, who consume these pastilles during Lent, and also to conserve the strength of their bell-ringers, is as thus: they reduce three cows to an Essence, which they do by boiling the cows and then placing the meats that are left in the pot through their presses and mangles until they are left with a solid weighing no more than 400 scruples [12 oz]. This they then place in a small cauldron containing 6 (what they call) etti [1 lb] of fine Sicilian sugar made by their Apothecary. And this they then boil together until it thickens and reduces and becomes an Essence. And then they convey the cauldron to the topmost part of the Priory and with a wooden spoon throw it drop by drop on to a marble slab placed on the ground beneath them and where it forms into Pastilles. And these are what they consume during Lent, and also use to conserve the strength of their bell-ringers. And they tell me there is enough nutriment in such a Pastille that a person may survive for three days without any other foods but only with water. And now I am set to ask the Prior whether he could also reduce six sheep to make a Sheep Pastille, and six Pigs to make a Pig Pastille, and the legs of 200 Frogs to make a Frog Pastille. I am thinking of My Lord Lodovico's soldiery and how they could benefit from such and not have to carry cows and pigs in their train when on their marches.

Donkey Omelette

Keep all your bad eggs to break in a bowl, beat them with a little rancid honey and cumin seed before cooking and place before your donkeys with their morning grasses.

Cow Cakes
(*or Ox Cubes*)

Immerse a cow – or ox – in a large boiler containing three carrots and a handful of juniper berries for such time – 15 or 16 hours normally – as all the meat drops off the bones. Place this meat in the cow press to extract all its juices. These you pour into flat pans and leave to co-agulate and when quite dried cut up into thumb-sized cubes which may then add to your boiling vegetables and so enrich them with the goodness of ox or cow without the inconvenience of killing a fresh ox or cow.

The cow juice left in your boiler may also be used. Drain it through a fine horsehair-sieve and use this to enrich your next boiling of turnips and sprouts.

False Sausage (I)

If a pig should not be present to be made into a sausage, mix some porridge with pig-fat and spiced whortleberries and fill boiled cow's udders with the mixture.

False Sausage (II)

Select six goose-necks from your larder, bone them, boil them lightly, then stuff them with a mixture of finely-cut goose liver, carrots and truffles. Tie up with horse-hair and cook as you would an ordinary sausage. (The recipe of my friend Gallius Senesali.)

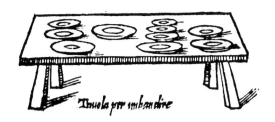

On the Qualities
of a Good Confectioner

Firstly, it must be a man, on account a woman's frame is unsuited to lifting great weights of marzipan.

Secondly, he should be clean and clear-skinned – for little is so off-putting to those about to eat his creations as a spotted confectioner, or one with long hairs which may have transferred themselves from his body into his confection.

And thirdly, he should have studied in architecture. For without a true knowledge of weights and stresses he cannot create confections which will stand on their own and not be liable to subsidence or even total collapse.

On a Disturbed Night
in Piacenza

The Osteria del Moro where Luca Pacioli and I did stay in
Piacenza I could not recommend even to a Barinese. At table
our first – and only – night they did serve us but lumps of
putrid cow-fat covered with a thick brown sauce that tasted
of the drains of Venice. Then there were fruits, some tainted
pears, some plums that had the wasp in, some shrivelled
grapes of yesteryear. And that was all, save cloudy wine.
The bed they gave me was but straw with lumps of dung – or
felt and smelt as such; for better comfort I did move its cover
to the floor and slept on it in much superior style. But there
was little peace, lewd fellows fighting down the stairs, and at
my next door a man was murdered – I heard his dying
screams; my notebooks and my purse I hid and placed a chest
against my door to avert same fate for me. Next time in
Piacenza I shall arrange to rest in Lord Visconti's house, and
others having business there I do advise to do the same.

On the Potential of
the Cornet

I am concerned that certain foods might be served in and
eaten from a cornet. Soup, instead of being poured on
wooden boards as at My Lord Lodovico's table, might
benefit from such a container – and his table, too. What
should the cornet be made of though? Of marzipan? Of
porridge? Or should it be of wood?

locanda

ghiottela

piastrella

Little Platter
of Trout's Intestines

Take the insides of a trout and clean them very well – at the
least four separate washings under running waters. Remove
what you do not like from them and mix the remainder with
a little pepper, parsley, bread-crumbs and hen-egg, and
spread on a crispy porridge. My friend Gaudio Affan di
Rivan considers this to be the most thoroughly disgusting
dish he has ever tasted, but I myself have a softness for it
along with the people of Ostia whose creation it is.

Oysters

Oysters taste best when cooked in the half-shell over charcoal – a little light oil sprinkled over them. The rich and
lustful who eat them raw do not know this.

Some Curious Facts
about Vinegar

Vinegar makes melancholic persons more melancholic, and
bleary-eyed persons more bleary-eyed. On the good side it
will cool you in hot weather if you dampen your wrists with
a mixture of it and decomposing grapes.

A List of Edible Insects

Crickets
Bees
Certain Caterpillars

And these are not edible:

Spiders
Earwigs
Large Flies

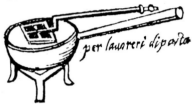

On the Preservation of Foodstuffs

I have been thinking of the preservation of foodstuffs, in particular of the preservation of frogs. Especially since I did hear of one Leoni Buillarotti by Lake Transimeno who each year herds many hundreds of his frogs on to the lake as it freezes, and is then able by sawing the ice in which they become frozen to eat of fresh frog throughout the months of Winter – though only the legs he says are the edible parts for human consumption and of the legs by far the most desirable portions are the fingers. Indeed by Lake Transimeno and down even unto the provinces of Rome, Leoni Buillarotti's frozen frog fingers are among the most covetted of dinner dishes each Winter. The legs, he says, should be peeled and steamed, then lightly marinated in a mixture of basilica, garlic and sprout-water before this consumption takes place; only then, Leoni Buillarotti advises, should the fingers be removed. Thirty to forty frog-fingers, he says, make a sufficient portion suited to a nobleman, whilst others at the table may be quite content with the remainder of the legs. The rest of the frog, he adds, he makes into cakes for the consumption of his cattle – though I myself have also heard of frog-cakes, heavily surrounded by the strongest-smelling perfumes, being carved into the likenesses of whole frogs and used as table decorations at the weddings of peasants in Puglia.

And now I am considering the application of Leoni Buillarotti's method of preservation to the preserving of sprouts and cows and other foodstuffs. I would cover the surface of a freezing lake with dead cows and sprouts and as the water froze solid over them then I would saw them up into individual blocks and transport them to caverns underground for safe keeping – thus enabling sprout-lovers to eat to their liking at any time of the year even during those months when sprouts are not being harvested, and those dedicated to cow-meat to savour it without the bother and delay of slaughtering a new one.

The advantage in preserved frogs and other preserved foodstuffs is that one is not dependent upon the seasons.

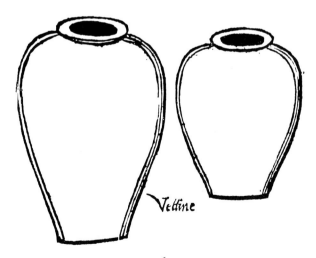

Vettine

Marcaiola

On the Most Beneficial Quantities of Foods and Liquids to be Consumed Each Day

As in all things living the substance of the body exceeds that which is liquid in it by a proportion of two and a half to one (my friend Benedetto Garvi's calculation) so should the amount of solid food fed to the body exceed the liquid by two and a half times. And to calculate the amounts needed for each individual then, as a well-packed bladder with intestines is adjudged the same weight as that of the human head, the amount of food and liquid to be consumed by the individual each day should equal the weight of his head – which in a full-grown person my friend Benedetto Garvi assures me is one seventh of his whole body weight. And thus if a man's head should weight 30 ettos [15 lbs] he should eat 20 ettos of solid food (porridge, olives and frogs legs – or such other variety of foods as he is able in his position to obtain) and 10 of liquid each day (bearing in mind that half of all porridges are liquid).

ON THE ABOVE

Upon deliberation I think I may be very wrong on this matter. I shall return to it.

On a Balanced Selection of Foodstuffs

There is no one foodstuff that a man could live on and survive were that the only foodstuff in the world; no one crop, no one berry, no one root, nor any one meat nor the milk of any one animal.

Nor are there any two foodstuffs that without any others would enable survival.

But there are three foodstuffs that a man could live on beneficially if he could obtain no others; and they are porridge, olives, and the legs of frogs. In this proportion should they be consumed:

> Seven tenths of porridge
> Two tenths of olives
> And two of the legs of frogs*

My friend Benedetto Garvi, with whom I discussed these proportions during many evenings, had been putting them into practise for nearly six months at the time of his unfortunate demise.

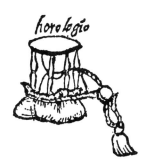

Time and time again in making the simplest of calculations Leonardo would err mathematically as here – and then always be too involved in his next project ever to have the time to revise the last and discover its errors.

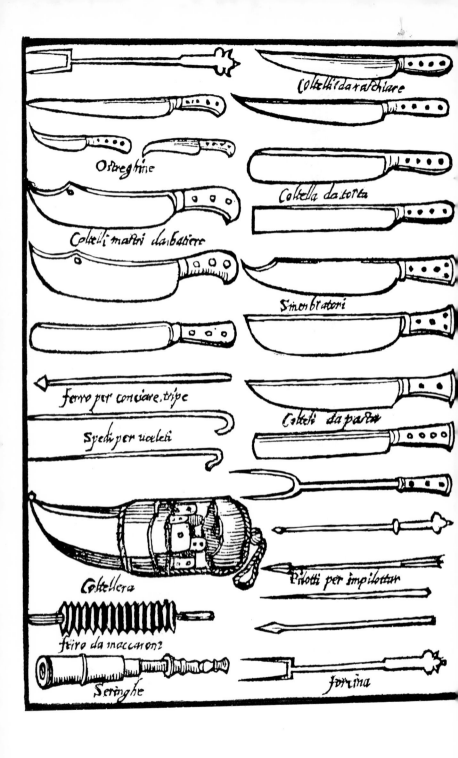

Coltelli da raschiare

Ostreghine

Coltella da torta

Coltelli maistri da batiere

Smorbiatori

ferro per conciare tripe

Coltelli da parar

Spedi per uceleti

Coltellera

Pilotti per impilottar

fero da maccaroni

Seringhe

forcina

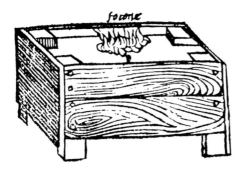

fo come

Further Observations upon some Vegetables and their Various Properties

❀ BROAD BEANS ❀

The ancients thought that inside broad beans were the souls of the dead and shunned the eating of them. This is not why I turn my back on them but because I have discovered these beans stimulate lecherousness, provoke sleeplessness and leave you swollen with wind.

❀ LENTILS ❀

The way to avoid billiosness from eating lentils is to cook them two times – throw away the waters in which you first cook them, then add vinegar and herbs to the waters for the second cooking. Even so, these lentils are not good for your chest, your brain or your sight.

❀ PEAS ❀

Peas are less harmful than beans, but beware of eating too many. Over-indulgence in peas can produce madness.

❀ CHICKPEAS ❀

The waters that you soak your chickpeas in may be drunk to purify your kidneys, crush your gallstone, and rid you of the worms in your stomach.

❀ LEEKS ❀

There are some who say leeks are an aphrodisiac and should be consumed on the wedding night. There are others who say leeks cure drunkenness. And yet others who claim leeks make the perfect laxative. That may be, but I say that eating leeks is wrong. Leeks give you a headache, ruin your teeth and gums, and are harmful to your eyesight. This is why I am determined to give up leek-eating.

❀ ONIONS ❀

The proper way (which many seem to have forgotten) to eat an onion is to cook it under ashes or charcoal; then, when cold, cut it into small pieces and dress with salt, oil, vinegar and grape or pear juice. (There are those who add pepper and cinnammon too.)

Eating too many onions will give you Heavy Head, will damage your memory, will make you sleepy, and give you disagreeable breath (the only antidote to which is to chew the roots of a beetroot).

Crushed onions you may place on your haemmeroids and they will be cured.

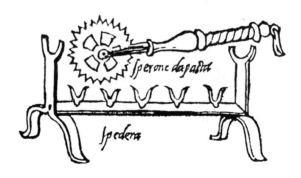

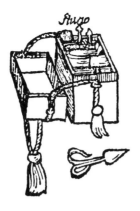

❊ GARLIC ❊

Garlic cooked with beans relieves coughing and breathlessness. Garlic crushed and laid around your room will keep away snakes, scorpions and other unwelcome small animals.

❊ TURNIP ❊

There are those who say there is nothing more harmful to the body than a turnip, that it causes swelling of the stomach, constipation and great irritability. They forget, perhaps, that a roasted turnip when mixed with pigfat and made into a paste and then spread on the foot will cure all blisters. And also they forget, perhaps, that the water from a boiled turnip when drunk alleviates the gouts. Also, a boiled turnip when mashed is one of the most favourite dishes of My Lord Lodovico.

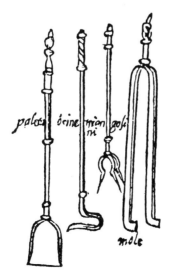

❀ THISTLES ❀

And just as there are those who say there is nothing more harmful to the body than a turnip, there are others who say that no day should pass without eating a thistle. They do not explain how or what part though. And I cannot imagine.

❀ RUNNER BEANS ❀

These are of little consequence either.

❀ CUCUMBER ❀

The seeds of the white cucumber put into sweet wine often prove helpful to women with bladdar troubles. But in others they produce only a bad humour and fevers. It is advisable to eat a cucumber, if you must eat a cucumber, without its skin or seeds, dressing it with a little salt, oil and vinegar.

❀ LUPINS ❀

When you have picked your lupins, expose them to the smoke of your fire for half a day before you chop them up and place them in the boiling pot. If they taste too bitter then they are best not eaten but rubbed on children's stomachs to combat vermin.

❀ FENNEL ❀

There is little to say about fennel, but for those who do not find it sweet enough my advice to them is, as winter approaches, to lay out the stalks on their floor and cover them with dung from the stables, and then the following year they will find it tastes much sweeter. I have heard of whole families dying from eating unsweet fennels so I believe this to be a reasonable precaution.

❀ PUMPKIN ❀

When it is still young and tender in the summer, in fact before it turns into the monstrous and obese thing it can become (and I have seen with my own eyes those that measure nine feet long) it should be peeled and cut into long slices which are dried in the sun and then can be used for food or the decoration of tables in winter.

❀ ELDER FLOWER ❀

The flower of the elder tree is especially good for those with dropsy. The berry, with which we dye our white hairs, is also, when cooked, effective against snake-bites. And the waters that the leaves have been cooked in may be sprinkled around the house to keep fleas away.

❀ SPINACH, PARSNIPS, BEETROOTS, ❀ CAULIFLOWERS, MUSHROOMS, TRUFFLES ❀ AND PANSIES ❀

All of these I am planning to write on later.

Conserva con mercantie